Designing for the Theatre

Second edition

Francis Reid

Routledge
Taylor & Francis Group
New York London

This edition published 2011 by Routledge:

Routledge
Taylor & Francis Group
711 Third Avenue
New York, NY 10017

Routledge
Taylor & Francis Group
2 Park Square, Milton Park
Abingdon, Oxon OX14 4RN

Second edition 1996
Reprinted 2000
First edition 1989
A & C Black (Publishers) Limited
35 Bedford Row, London WC1R 4JH

© 1996, 1989 Francis Reid

ISBN 0-7136-4398-6

Published simultaneously in the USA by
Theatre Arts Books/Routledge
29 West 35 Street, New York, NY 10001

ISBN 0-87830-062-7

CIP catalogue records for this book are available
from the British Library and the Library of
Congress.

CONTENTS

ACKNOWLEDGEMENTS

The author and publishers gratefully acknowledge permission to use the following:

pp. 5, 8 Richard Leacroft, *Theatre & Playhouse*, Methuen; p. 6 RHWL, architects, courtesy of Town House Publicity (photo: Martin Charles); p. 10 courtesy of Rockerick Ham; p. 11 Orange County Performing Arts Center; pp. 12–13 *New York Times*; p. 14 Theatre Projects Consultants, p. 15 Royal Shakespeare Company (photo: Nicholas Sargeant); p. 16 (photo: Michael Mayhew); p. 17 RHWL, architects; p. 21 David Walker; p. 22 Jim Hiley *Theatre at Work*, Routledge & Kegan Paul (photo: Zoe Dominic); pp. 25, 57, 58, 59 Glyndebourne (photos: Guy Gravett); p. 23 (photo: Ivan Kyncl); p. 26 (photo: Donald Cooper); p. 27 (photo: Bill Cooper); p. 28 Royal Opera House (photo: Leslie E. Spatt); p. 29 (photo: Cathy Ryan); pp. 37, 38 Pani; p. 39 Prague Theatre Institute; p. 40 (photo: Ann Curtis); p. 44 Above (photo: Robert Workman), below (photo: Peter Davison); p. 45 (photo: Claire Lyth); p. 53 (right) David Hockney, *Hockney Paints the Stage*; p. 61 (illustrations: Rae Smith); p. 65 (illustrations: Kate Borthwick); p. 68 (illustration: Paul Dart); p 70 Wimbledon School of Art; pp. 78, 79 Modelbox Limited (photo: TVS); p. 87 Central School of Art & Design.

PROLOGUE

Theatre has always been a strongly visual experience. But the images which once merely decorated the stage are today expected to be a totally integrated feature of the production, not only providing environmental support for the actors but contributing a visual response that is metaphorical rather than literal.

This book considers the potential contribution of costume, settings, props and lighting to a stage production and endeavours to explain the process by which they are designed. Theatre design, like every other art, is ultimately based on decisions which arise from inspiration rather than logic. Yet these ideas can only be stimulated, filtered and developed within the framework of a work process.

The book is intended as an introduction to the possibilities and processes of design for the theatre. It is hoped it will offer sufficient insight into the design process to provide an embryonic designer with a method of proceeding from first thought to first night.

The author is indebted to the many designers with whom he has worked — and the many more he has never met but whose art has excited him as a member of the audience — for stimulating his visual thinking about theatre. He is particularly grateful to London's Central School of Art and Design, whose theatre design staff and students inspired this attempt to verbalise a process which is concerned with images rather than with words.

Although its basic work processes tend to remain constant, theatre design is a continuously evolving art. The illustrations in this new edition, therefore, include many designs for productions which have been staged in the seven years since the first edition was published. These designs were shown in the *Make Space!* exhibition from which the British entry was selected for the 1995 Prague Quadrennial where it was awarded a special Gold Medal.

1 THE ROLE OF DESIGN

THEATRE DESIGNERS are members of the creative team who bring life, through performance, to a dramatic script and/or score. This team includes:

- *Actors* who are the primary interpreters of a writer's words and music.

- *Designers* whose visual interpretation of script and score costumes the actors and provides a supportive environment.

- *Directors* who integrate all the individual elements of interpretation within an overall concept, the style of which they have primary responsibility for establishing.

- *Audiences* who assist a fresh renewal of the interpretation at each performance through their response to the production and their interactive rapport with the actors and with each other.

Whether *writers* and *composers* take an active role in the interpretation of their work depends primarily, and obviously, upon whether they are still alive. Even so, their involvement rarely extends beyond the first production and possibly an occasional major revival.

A large support team of *enablers* help translate creative ideas into performance reality. In particular, the realisation of all visual aspects is dependent upon the interpretative skills of costume, set and prop makers, and technicians.

The prime enablers are *producers* whose packaging of a production includes the decision to do it, the bringing together of a team and the provision of funding. The producer's role is essentially one of creative midwifery. During preparation and rehearsals the key enablers are *production managers* whose organisation of time and money ensures that the production is ready for its first performance, on schedule and within budget. Responsibility for enabling a smooth performance every night, through the integration of acting and technology, rests with *stage managers*.

It must be emphasised that every member of the enabling team has a creative role. Designers are totally dependent upon the creative skills of all those who are involved in interpreting their designs. Interpretation is more than just a matter of carrying out instructions. Even the most detailed design is still something of a skeletal idea to be developed and transformed during its realisation as a costume, prop, scenic element or lighting balance.

Indeed at no point during the realisation of a dramatic work for performance can anyone respond in a merely passive way. Even when the script includes very specific instructions for how it is to be performed, and when these instructions are faithfully adhered to, the variations between different productions can still be immense. Therefore a designer's role, like that of everyone working in a theatre (or attending the performance as audience), is one of creative interpretation.

THE DESIGNER'S VISUAL RESPONSE

The designer's contribution to a production arises out of a visual response to the dramatist's words and/or the composer's music. This response will be influenced by discussions with the other members of the creative team. Ideally it would also be a response to observation of character and ensemble development during rehearsal. However, the realities of scheduling normally require irreversible design decisions to be made before rehearsals have even started.

This visual response will most obviously manifest itself in the costuming of the actors and provision of an environment for the stage action. But it should also offer a statement about the play's intent: a visual metaphor for its verbal philosophy.

This philosophy may not necessarily be a particularly deep or searching one. Theatre offers the possibility of exploring the nature of humanity at all levels, from the fundamental to the frivolous. And to make comment on several levels simultaneously. Even the most lightweight play, apparently seeking only to amuse, offers comment on human frailty that can trigger quite fundamental thinking in an audience.

The designer's visual response to the nature of the play will be a factor which both influences, and is influenced by, the style of production which the creative team decide to pursue. Visual style will help to determine the nature of the stage environment. But this will also be heavily dependent upon the practical needs of the action. Design should be focused on the need to support the actors: the clothes they wear, the objects they handle and the world they inhabit must support their projection of the characters they play.

AREAS OF DESIGN

Costumes including wigs and make-up, are particularly associated with acting since the clothes an actor wears will both stem from the way a character is played and, in turn, influence the way that the character is played.

Settings and lighting provide a flexible stage environment which can support the play's progress through time and place. The nature and flexibility of this stage environment is determined by the demands of the text, and by the way in which the chosen production style handles such demands.

Props contribute a link between actor and environment. All objects which the actors handle are classified as props (shortened from properties, a word deeply established in theatre jargon). They are an intrinsic part of the action and are not to be confused with dressing the set by placing objects on it for purely visual effect. Props include everything from furniture and meals to the personal props used by particular characters in the furtherance of the plot (e.g. pens, letters, money, etc.) and costume props which are more in the nature of clothing accessories (e.g. umbrellas, spectacles, etc.).

VISUAL STYLE

Everything placed upon a stage by a designer is conditioned by the visual style which has been adopted for the production. This visual style contributes to, and is derived from, the overall production style which the creative team have chosen for their interpretation of the script. It determines just how the designer dresses the actors and provides them with a stage environment. Conversely, it is the way in which the actors are dressed and the nature of the environment in which they perform that establishes the style. A classic case of interaction!

FOUR-DIMENSIONAL DESIGN

Theatre designers are neither interior designers nor fashion designers. Stage space, stage clothes and stage lighting are not designed for living in, but to provide a visual metaphor for a literary or musical dramatic work and support its communication through performance.

At a purely physical level the theatre designer, handling three-dimensional space and objects within a time progression, is a four-dimensional designer. However, considering the somewhat metaphysical nature of theatre, it would not be difficult to propose additional, more philosophically based, dimensions to a theatre designer's work.

2 THE THEATRE BUILDING

Before considering production design in any depth, we should give some thought to the nature of theatre buildings. How does the design of a production's stage environment relate to the total environment provided by the architectural form and function of the theatre in which the production is housed?

Until the present century, the situation was straightforward. Theatre had a standard form and, although this gradually developed, the pace of change was so slow that each generation had a clear view of what constituted a theatre. And they could go to a performance with a clear expectation of a standard production style, familiar in both its acting and its settings.

But in the current century the pace of change has quickened. 'Theatre' has been the subject of a great deal of fundamental thinking, and there is now a whole range of theatre building forms simultaneously available as options. Perhaps the easiest way to consider these current optional forms is by a brief historical survey of their evolution.

FROM THE RENAISSANCE TO THE EARLY TWENTIETH CENTURY

Changeable scenery did not become a regular part of the actor's environment until the development of indoor theatre after the Renaissance. And then, for nearly two centuries, the scenery remained a decorative background with little interaction between actor and scene.

Actors in a Georgian playhouse played on a stage which thrust into the auditorium, well beyond the first boxes. Any action of consequence took place forward of the proscenium which was flanked by a pair of doors used for entrances and exits. The close contact with the audience that resulted from this thrusting stage was further emphasised by actors and audience sharing the same auditorium lighting. The actors were thus associated more with the galleried room that was the auditorium than with the scenic background which was restricted to making a pictorial statement of the location of the action.

Although the scenic pictures were not a particularly integrated feature of a production, they did have an important role and indeed their significance for the audience is confirmed by the printing of descriptions on the advertising bills, especially when a scene was newly painted. (A playhouse repertoire was so wide that the basic production design process was one of permutation. New scenes were additions to stock, and although a scene's initial appearance might well be

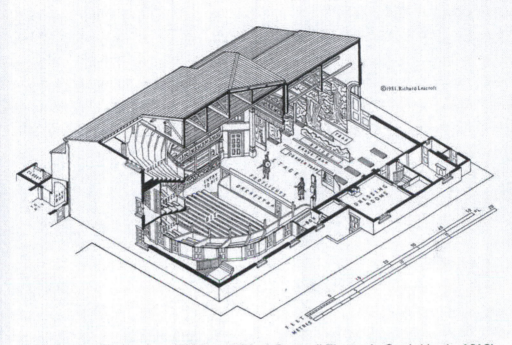

Richard Leacroft's drawing of William Wilkins' *Barnwell Theatre in Cambridge* (c. 1816) reconstructs a typical intimate Georgian playhouse.

for a specific play, thereafter it could be called upon to serve any production.)

Audiences responded positively to perspective painting in a theatre where stage depth could be used to enhance the perspective. We cannot fully know how the audiences reacted but it seems likely that their objective appreciation of the painter's art was mixed with a suspension of disbelief which, induced by the total atmosphere of the performance, allowed paint and canvas to become reality.

Scenic backgrounds were always accorded more importance in opera and ballet — and indeed still are. Large choruses, and plots hinging upon magic transformations, brought the action into a more integral contact with the scene. But that scene was still a perspective painting whose vanishing point resulted in perfect viewing being possible from only one central position in the auditorium. Nevertheless, the general quality of the painting was such that pleasure could usually be obtained from even the most awkward line of sight.

It was audience preference for a visual theatre that ultimately pushed the actor back into the scene. The managers were happy to accede: apart from a commercial desire (and need) to please the audience, the retreat of the thrust stage increased auditorium capacity.

Scenery took the standardised form imposed by the universal technical architecture of the stage. This provided machinery for locating and changing side wings and overhead borders. Every stage had sets of grooves in which side wings could be slid on and off. The grooves were parallel to the front of the stage and

In Frank Matcham's *Theatre Royal in Newcastle* (1901, restored by RHWL, architects, in 1987), deep balconies offer most of the audience a clear, although for many a distant, sightline to a stage which has retreated behind the proscenium frame.

arranged in groups to permit rapid scene changing by replacing one set of wings with another. Changes on the simplest stages were effected by sliding the wings in surface grooves, but in more elaborate theatres, the wings were mounted through the stage floor on a complex system of carriages whose travel could be simultaneously controlled by a capstan.

Space above the stage was restricted to the minimum required for changing shallow borders, although the more elaborate theatres also had machinery for lowering chariots to carry the gods upon whom so many opera plots depended for resolution. Stage height restrictions were such that any cloths had to be rolled or 'tumbled' by raising them in sections; in Britain the rear of the scene was normally a pair of scenic flats, or 'back-shutters', which slid on from the side to join at the centre.

The continual need to maximise the financial capacity of the house became the major influence in architectural developments, particularly in Britain where public subsidy did not become available until the middle of the present century. In central Europe, the civic theatres which grew out of the court theatre tradition were able to retain shallow balconies with a maximum of three or four rows of seats allowing a good contact with the stage, even if the side seats had a restricted area of vision. In Britain, however, the Georgian stage's intimate contact with pit, boxes and gallery was lost when the Victorian theatre developed deep shelves of stalls and overhanging balconies. Certainly there were fewer side seats with restricted view, but a large proportion of the audience were now a long way from the stage and their loss of contact was increased by the tunnelling effect of the overhang of the deep balconies.

Differences also affected the stage and the ancillary spaces for both actors and audience. European cities accorded their theatres large prime sites. In Britain particularly, but also to some considerable extent in the New World, commercial developers were forced by economics to use sites that were small and irregular in shape. The resulting theatres were (or rather *are* since many remain in active use) often miracles of clever architectural planning, but the size and shape of their stages place a considerable strain on the ingenuity of today's designers who have to use them for production styles very different from those for which they were originally built.

The Victorian stage developed an advanced technology for presenting highly visual productions with changing scenery. The roof over the stage was raised to provide a tower into which full sized cloths could be hoisted. The stage floor was traversed by a series of sloats (narrow slots running the full width of the stage) through which two-dimensional pieces of scenery could rise and fall. Between the sloats were a series of wider sections which could open to form traps, or provide elevators for making levels and raising large pieces of scenery and groups of actors. There was very little wing space, and most scene docks were limited to the storage of flat scenery.

Thus the stage was geared to one particular visual style: a pictorial realism painted on canvases which were limited by standard machinery to being positioned parallel to the front of the stage. Depth could be achieved by the relative

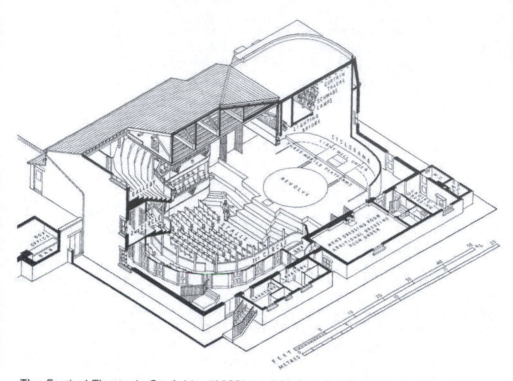

The *Festival Theatre in Cambridge* (1926) combined two of the major directions of inter-war experiments: removal of the proscenium, and the use of a cyclorama in association with directional spotlighting of the actors to explore fresh possibilities in controlling stage space. (The Festival Theatre was an adaptation of the Georgian Barnwell Theatre: compare this Richard Leacroft drawing with that on p. 5).

placing of these two-dimensional elements, but a third dimension was also normally incorporated in the painting.

Although developments in lighting, particularly the intensely bright directional beams of the limelights, were beginning to introduce a further element of space and time control, the overall contribution of design was still that of a decorative background which strove for an illusion — usually romanticised — of reality. The actor's environment might now be changeable in more sophisticated ways, but it was virtually still the same combination of painted canvas cloths, wings and borders which had been developed very soon after theatre first moved indoors.

THE TWENTIETH CENTURY

This was the situation at the beginning of the twentieth century, and the years leading up to the 1914 war were the last era when the word *theatre* — whether applied to the building or to the productions on its stage — implied any kind of standardised predictable experience. The second half of the nineteenth century had seen an increasing questioning of the established theatre style with its rhetorical acting and pictorial painting. Whether it was Ibsen seeking a greater naturalism or Appia and Craig seeking to abandon any attempt at reproducing reality, a new theatre of many co-existing styles was on the way.

From 1920 the pace quickened. At first the changes had to take place within the format of existing theatre buildings. The stages of central Europe were fitted with huge dome cycloramas to back non-representational scenery with an impression of boundless space. There were experiments with such devices as revolves and castored wagons.

In the smaller theatres in particular, there were attempts to break down the framing effect of the proscenium which tended to distance the actors from the audience. This was something of a return towards the intimacy of the Georgian playhouse, although now the acting style required that the scenic environment also thrust through the proscenium rather than remain a mere background. However, this kind of experimental activity, although highly significant for the future, formed a minute proportion of the audience's theatre experience. Proscenium-framed three-dimensional realism became the standard for plays while the art of the painter flourished in ballet.

The overwhelming architectural influence was the cinema. Clear sightlines from all seats to the stage. Rarely more than one balcony. Exuberant baroque plaster decoration swept away to be replaced by restrained art deco plaster relief, often diffusely lit from concealed coves. This movement made little impression on opera houses in the German and Italian traditions, but elsewhere it became something of an international style.

In the surge of new theatre building immediately after the Second World War, architects were briefed to combine pure sightline with a proscenium so unstressed that it would form only a minimal barrier between actor and audience. The proscenium became, rather than a conscious frame, the natural termination of the auditorium walls and ceiling. Slots and bridges were incorporated in these walls and ceilings to accommodate the massive growth in lighting as a major component of the stage environment. An elevator immediately forward of the proscenium could drop to provide an orchestra pit or rise to form a thrusting apron stage, although such a thrust is somewhat token in any but the smallest theatre.

There was a growing realisation through the 1970s that theatres with pure cinematic sightlines ceased to be effective above about four or five hundred seats. When the entire audience is placed centrally with a clear view of the stage, the volume of auditorium required to accommodate a particular size of audience increases very quickly. Furthermore, the members of that audience become isolated from one another. In the anxiety to improve the actor-audience relationship, the necessity for an audience to gel and become more than the sum of its parts (the audience-audience relationship) had been somewhat forgotten. With people in side boxes an audience tends to be aware of one another and it becomes easier to make a corporate response, especially to comedy. Moreover, blank walls increase any actor-audience barrier whereas boxes can help form a bridge. And with people hanging on the walls, more of the audience can be closer to the stage,

The 1969 *Thorndike Theatre at Leatherhead* is an intimate single tier playhouse (520 seats) where the stage is framed by the natural termination of the auditorium walls and ceiling. (Architect: Roderick Ham).

although some of them have a poor sightline to it. A balance has to be struck between contact and field of vision: this is currently the major area of concern in deciding the architectural form of new theatres.

British theatres

In Britain, the main surge of theatre building was the 1960s' and 1970s' chain of regional playhouses. Each has its own acting company and production facilities to present one play at a time within a three week cycle of simultaneous preparation, rehearsal and performance. Most of these theatres have a seating capacity of five or six hundred seats which can be accommodated within a single tier offering a good sightline to, and contact with, the stage. Virtually no large scale theatres were built, and the nation's stock of such theatres was allowed to run down with near disastrous consequences for housing the performances of major works of music theatre. However, the redevelopment of these theatre sites was halted just in time to keep a barely adequate circuit of refurbished old theatres which can receive, with both technical difficulty and audience discomfort, tours of large scale musicals and national opera and dance productions.

A theatre with 3000 seats has to be very large, especially if each seat is to have a clear sightline to the stage. And there can be acoustic problems arising from the distance which lateral sound reflections have to travel from the side walls to the centre seats. California's *Orange County Performing Arts Center* inserts mid-auditorium walls to divide the audience space into smaller acoustic units.

Central European theatres

After the war devastation of central European cities, particularly in Germany, the reinstatement of theatres was accorded a very high priority. Most of these theatres work in the repertoire mode with several productions simultaneously available for permutation to give a varying nightly performance schedule. With a strongly operatic tradition (West Germany alone has over 80 civic theatres, of which some 50 perform opera) the city theatres in small towns have a company capable of presenting evenings of opera, musical, dance and drama. The city's orchestra plays in the pit and gives symphony concerts on the stage. As cities become bigger, the drama and opera/dance performances are given on separate stages.

Such repertoire theatres require extensive stage space and technical facilities to accommodate the twice daily changeovers between different performances and rehearsals. And the staffing levels for performers and supporting personnel require budgets only dreamed of outside the central European tradition. These new

The *Metropolitan Opera House in New York's Lincoln Center* is fully mechanised, in the German tradition, to handle a repertoire programme changing daily.

1 Lighting bridges.
2 Border lights.
3 Flying bars.
4 Auditorium chandeliers.
5 Auditorium ceiling lighting bridges.
6 Auditorium.
7 Proscenium lighting towers, mobile to vary stage width.
8 Control desks for flying and stage machinery.
9 Stage manager's control desk.
10 Orchestra pit.
11 Main stage (30m wide, 25m deep, 100ft × 83ft) comprising seven hydraulic elevators. (Elevators 1–3 are double-decked and can rise to 8.5m (28ft) exposing a complete scene pre-set on lower deck.)
12 Side wagon stage, 18m × 14.5m (60ft × 48ft), can transport a complete scene on to the main stage area.
13 Personnel elevator.
14 Offices and staff rooms.
15 Scenery and prop storage.
16 Rehearsal studios.
17 Props and small scenery lift between stage and storage.
18 Elevator for transporting rolled cloths (up to 20.7m (68ft) long) between stage and storage.
19 Rear wagon stage, 18m × 18m (60ft × 60ft), with 17.5m (58ft) diameter revolve.
20 Loading dock accommodating four trucks simultaneously.
21 Dressing rooms.
22 Elevator between stage and dressing rooms.
23 Wardrobe for current repertoire.
24 Costume workshop.
25 Main scenery lift, 7.5m × 8.2m (25ft × 27ft), between stage and storage.
26 Left wagon stage, 18m × 12m (60ft × 40ft).
27 Sound isolating door to permit scene changes on side wagon stage while performance continues on main stage.
28 Cyclorama unrolling on track to surround stage to a height of 33m (109ft).
29 & 30 Construction shops.
31 Paint shop.

The 460 seat *Martha Cohen Theatre* in the Calgary Centre for the Performing Arts in Canada is a typical example of the current trend in returning to theatre forms which seek to maximise an audience's corporate identity and its contact with the stage, even if this gives some of the seats a less than pure sightline. (Architect: Joel Barnett, with Theatre Projects Consultants).

theatres were given large stages with extensive technical facilities for preparing, storing and moving large operatic settings within a complex schedule. The standard became a cruciform layout with side and rear wagon stages which can be rolled on to the main stage while carrying complete settings. The main stage is a combination of elevators, sectionalised to provide levels and rake options. An inner proscenium frame, carrying overhead lighting bridges and side lighting platforms, can be adjusted to provide alternative sizes of framing.

Very few of these theatres forgot the need to hang the audience on the walls. The desirability of improving sightlines was acknowledged and so, in most cases, although the boxes were retained, they were re-orientated to face more towards the stage. Maximum seating could be held at around just over a thousand because commercial pressures did not demand a sacrifice of the quality of audience experience.

American theatres
Commercial pressures are probably strongest in America. The Broadway theatres of the earlier part of the century solved this reasonably successfully by going for a

The stage of the Royal Shakespeare Company's *Swan Theatre* (Michael Reardon & Associates, 1986) at Stratford-upon-Avon thrusts deeply into the auditorium. Shallow galleries surround the stage on three sides, allowing all 430 members of the audience to have a very close contact with the actors.

wide auditorium which brought a large proportion of a large audience close to the stage — particularly good for musicals, less so for drama. But the subsequent need to increase capacity, coupled with a devoted commitment to the pursuit of pure sightline, produced many cavernous theatres where a large proportion of the audience are not just remote but positively isolated from the stage. It is surprising just how lonely one can be in a huge theatre of this kind. Consequently, in the last decade or so, new theatre building in America has demonstrated an accelerating trend towards rediscovery of the contact advantages of hanging audience on the side walls.

Proscenium theatres

For proscenium theatres, therefore, the search continues for that elusive ideal compromise between good sight and good contact in a large auditorium. The stage is perhaps less of a problem: most designers would opt for maximum unencumbered space with a minimum of permanent machinery. The usefulness of such machinery is acknowledged on a stage with an intensive repertoire. But a fixed installation can hinder rather than help development of an ever-widening range of production styles. Unencumbered space leaves the designer free to choose an appropriate technical palette.

The growing sophistication of proscenium theatres with their elaborate technology has provoked, inevitably, a reaction from those who feel that such a

The *National Theatre's Cottesloe* is a neutral box studio with permanent courtyard-style galleries on the walls. It has been successful in most forms and particularly so in developing a promenade style of performance where acting and audience areas shift and mingle as the play progresses. (Bill Bryden's production of *Candleford*, designed by William Dudley.)

building comes between actor and audience. They seek a return to simpler forms of staging where the drama can make a more direct impact.

Alternatives to the proscenium

Down with the proscenium! has been a twentieth century cry that peaked during the 1960s and led to theatres being built in alternative forms. To allow a larger proportion of the audience to come into closer contact with the actors requires the stage to thrust into the audience, even to be encircled by it. Therefore, thrust stages and theatres-in-the-round have been two of the major forms resulting from total removal of the proscenium. Other forms that encompass this philosophy range from end-staging, where the audience face the actors but the stage has no proscenium frame, to promenade performances with the action moving to different points within a shared space where the audience ebb and flow to make

At *Northampton's Derngate Centre* sections of the auditorium, such as this triple-tier unit of boxes complete with access corridors, can be moved around on air castors enabling the 1400 seat theatre to change rapidly and effectively between opera, ballet and musicals, arena, concert and flat floor formats.

space for the actors. Such performance forms have been developed by 'fringe' or 'alternative' companies experimenting in small theatres adapted from found spaces.

It has also become standard practice for mainstream theatre companies working in their own building to have a small experimental studio as a secondary playing space. For this, the black box form became very fashionable for a time in the 1960s and 1970s. This is a neutral space which can adapt to any form. Some attempts were made to provide flexibility by installations of complex machinery to vary the actor/audience playing relationship. But it was found that arrangements which in theory offered unlimited flexibility imposed limitations in practice: after all, the nature of experiment is that the outcome is not known in advance. So, most studio theatres were simple neutral spaces (often black) with an overall lighting grid and seating units to be placed anywhere.

In theory such an empty neutral space should stimulate fresh imaginative thinking but in reality a stronger stimulus seems to be provided by the challenge of responding to, or reacting against, something tangible. Many of the black boxes soon settled down into a semi-permanent form, evolved from the proportions of the room and its access points, and rarely changed because of the labour costs in effecting a rearrangement. Consequently there has been a move to design studio theatres which are flexible yet have a definite form which favours certain arrangements. Also there is a tendency to move away from black which, although neutral, inevitably burdens any production with more than just a hint of gloom and doom.

With so many varieties of mainstream and alternative theatre coexisting, the second half of the twentieth century has become the first era without a standard form of theatre building. Performances can be housed anywhere, from street corners to computerised palaces of sophisticated technology.

The multi-purpose theatre

In response to this situation, there has been a search for a multi-purpose theatre building which would adapt to meet the requirements of all sorts of performance scales and styles from opera to drama and from proscenium to thrust. Alas, such buildings have to include so much compromise that they are rarely satisfactory even in their main form. However, there are signs that new technology may allow a greater freedom to adapt performance spaces of all sizes. The air castor enables quite chunky bits of an auditorium, such as seating blocks and even wall sections (including those carrying audience boxes) to be moved, hovercraft fashion, with little physical effort. The particular advantage of the air castor is that, unlike any mechanism involving wheels, the castored units are rock solid once they are in position and the air cushion has been removed.

DESIGNING FOR A PARTICULAR THEATRE

However, very few theatres can offer any significant flexibility in form, auditorium decoration or stage facilities. The designer of any production therefore has to acknowledge the strengths and weaknesses of the particular theatre in which it will be housed. This can be difficult for a production intended to tour a wide range of theatres (a problem discussed in Chapter 5), but the designer and the rest of the production team are usually able to give the necessary essential consideration to the architectural form of the theatre where the performances will take place — particularly its size, form, sightlines, actor/audience relationships and decorative style.

3 VISUAL STYLE

Just as there is no longer any standard style for theatre architecture, so also is there no standard style for staging a production. There is currently no orthodoxy which we can take as the point of departure for establishing a new style. Theatre has reached a development point where virtually anything goes. A point where a production's style is no longer expected to be either derivative of the past or based upon the logic of a new philosophy. The only requirement is internal consistency. Indeed, establishing internal consistency has become the principal means for establishing style. A production may take virtually any proposition as its starting point so long as the consequences of that starting point are followed through.

DEPARTURE FROM REALISM

A possible basis for any consideration of theatrical style is the extent and nature of its departure from realism. The mechanisms of performance, particularly the need for an actor to project a character rather than simply feel it, make true realism almost impossible to achieve on a stage. The nearest approach is a realism that is barely heightened.

On the other hand it is difficult for acting to depart a long way from natural behaviour. Most plays (and operas, ballets and musicals) are about human relationships. The performers are people acting people. Therefore their acting tends to have its roots in natural human behaviour.

Since acting style has these roots in realism, it is the visual elements that must make the boldest statements in a production. Although the costumes worn by the actors will need to be based to some considerable extent on real clothes, the departure of the scenic environment from the reality of nature can be almost total. But since actors are at the heart of any theatrical performance, we need to consider some basic aspects of acting style before discussing the visual contribution.

ACTING STYLE

Dance is probably the actor's furthest and most obvious departure from natural behaviour. While dancing can be a component of human behaviour, it is not one that is consistently used as a means of daily communication. With the loss of vocal language, dancers have to communicate with a body language, whether in ballet's classical traditions or in looser contemporary forms. And any form of dance is highly dependent upon atmospheric and emotional support from music.

Although the singer communicates with a vocal language, there is considerable difference from speech. The distancing, however, is somewhat dependent upon the nature of the music. The many notes to the bar of eighteenth century opera are closer to speech than the sustained vocal lines of much of the nineteenth century. And operas which have sung recitatives, or are through composed, have fewer problems of stylistic consistency than those which include spoken dialogue between the big arias and ensembles. Few musicals have completely abandoned spoken dialogue, but there has been a growing tendency in recent years for the songs to be more integral to the action so that they may carry the action forward rather than just comment upon what has happened or is about to happen. But perhaps music theatre's unique power lies in its potential for several characters to sing simultaneously, allowing a series of ideas and emotions to be superimposed rather than presented sequentially. This technique is so consistently deployed in operatic writing that it is automatically accepted, even expected, by audiences as a natural constituent of operatic acting style.

Music offers the theatre simultaneous freedom and constraints. There is a release from conforming to many of the more logical aspects of real human behaviour. But the music imposes a firm structure which controls the overall timing, allowing only subtle variations in pacing.

In drama, where spoken dialogue is the medium of communication, it is speech and movement which set the acting style. Taking natural (i.e. non-acting) behaviour as a base line, various acting techniques can be used to establish individual characters and project them. Exaggeration is the basic technique, and while this may possibly be an exaggeration of the total behaviour pattern, it is more likely to be a heightening of only certain aspects. Excessive exaggeration usually leads towards simplification of a character, and over simplified characters tend to become stereotypes or even caricatures.

It is a wish to communicate the subtleties of human behaviour that lies at the heart of the restrained near-natural acting styles which are the norm. Or are the norm in theatres whose priority is the interpretation of the details of the text rather than just the projection of its basic overall philosophy. On the other hand, theatres promoting a polemic message, often with political intent, project people as simple stereotypes and welcome the clarity which can stem from exaggerated behaviour.

The acting style may be a period one. It may be an attempt to recapture (perhaps heightening in the process) the behaviour of an earlier age or perhaps of an earlier theatre. Such historically based styles are difficult to promote since many experts disagree, and most audiences are unaware, of the details of such period behaviour. Indeed what we are offered is often based on rhetoric or insincerity or both.

So the acting style in spoken drama tends to be restricted to a small range of exaggerations of natural behaviour. This range extends from a realism that is positively but barely heightened to full caricature. Although the more pronounced degrees of exaggeration are perhaps more readily acceptable in comedy than in serious drama, it is difficult for actors to sustain any inwardly based truth in their performance if the acting style is broadened to the point of caricature.

But the key to a successful style is a consistency in these exaggerations which makes them credible: an essential factor in convincing an audience to suspend their disbelief. If all the actors behave in a consistent way, they are much more likely to be believed.

It is the small alternative theatres with a close audience contact who have been most able to explore acting styles. And their experiments with a closer integration of music, song and dance into a drama which in itself is based on a freer text have had considerable influence on the writing and production style of today's theatre. However, such experiments have only confirmed the need for an acting style which is rooted in real life but with just the right degree of heightening to ensure positive projection.

Period line and detail in David Walker's costume designs for the children in *Werther* are not only historically accurate but have been subtly strengthened and individualised in accord with the romanticism of Massenet's music and in support of the actors' character projection.

COSTUME STYLE

Clothes are the visual element most clearly supportive of the actor. A stage costume needs to be related to the clothes that the character would wear in real life. But, like the acting, the clothes will need to be at least a little larger than life. Even when the stage costumes for a contemporary play are selected from clothes designed and sold for street wear, the chosen items are likely to be at least slightly more emphatic than the character would choose. This is because costumes, like actors, have not merely to be in character but to project that character. The extent of their exaggeration will be geared to the degree with which the acting style departs from realism.

Reality heightened by selecting only significant items can often make an environment seem more natural than when every detail is included. (John Dexter's production of Brecht's *Galileo* at the National Theatre, designed by Jocelyn Herbert with lighting by Andy Phillips.)

When productions are set in an identifiable historic period, the clothes can offer major support through authenticity in their cut and detailing. In addition to their visual contribution, they can help the actors to develop a feel for period behaviour, particularly movement. However, period authenticity alone will not provide a visual style. Designing stage costumes requires an artist's eye to effect a transformation by making a selective heightening of the period reality. The extent of this transformation is often partly determined by the need to help bridge differences between an acting style, with roots firmly in a barely heightened version of natural behaviour, and a scenic environment that owes little to reality.

SCENIC ENVIRONMENT STYLE

The essential elements in a stage environment are space and time. Stage *space* defines appropriate areas for action. These areas not only position the actors so that their responses can be clearly seen, but also where they can establish a

For Stephen Daldry's production of Arnold Wesker's *The Kitchen*, Mark Thompson thrust the acting area out into the auditorium so that the apparent chaos of a commercial kitchen could be fully experienced by the audience. Lighting by Johanna Town.

Herr Puntila verlobt sich
mit den Frühaufsteherinnen

To ensure that the audience play a fully active role in a performance, Brecht required his designers to provide a stage environment incorporating visual elements which would remind the spectators that they were in a theatre. Andreas Reinhardt's design for Paul Dessaus's opera version of Brecht's *Puntilla* at the Deutsche Staatsoper, Berlin (directed by Ruth Berghaus) contains many of the characteristic Brecht features (including representational and graphic elements, visible wires for a half curtain, clear even light) which have influenced much of today's visual approach to staging.

rapport with the audience. The space is structured, perhaps just by its shape, possibly with levels, so that actors' positions can be manipulated to point changing relationships between characters as the plot develops. And the importance that dramatic structure tends to place upon entrances and exits is likely to require that these points of access to the acting area be emphasised.

An example of heightened romanticism, a style so abhorred by Brecht but a valid approach to Puccini. (Michael Redgrave's Glyndebourne production of *La Bohème* with sets by Henry Bardon, costumes by David Walker and lighting by Francis Reid.)

Just how much the space is identified as a specific place is a matter at the very root of style. Space may be given identity in all sorts of ways from total pictorial structuring to the presence of one simple but significant object. Space may be defined mainly by light and an indication of its place given by the quality of that light. Or the location may be allowed to spring purely from the actors' words. However, it is but a hairsbreadth that separates supporting the actors and exposing them. Actors in the centre of a bare stage have the total attention of their audience; but although there is no potential visual distraction there is also no support. A well designed stage setting never distracts and is finely balanced between support and exposure.

Acting areas should have sufficient credibility for the audience to believe that the action could take place there. Or, at the very least, not be confused to the extent of having their concentration diverted because they feel a need to supply their own rationalisation.

Stage *time* is not real time. It very rarely conforms to the time span of the

The Swan Theatre (page 15) became a dilapidated opera house for the RSC production of *The Beggar's Opera*. Using additional balconies on seemingly insubstantial supports and makeshift staircases apparently lashed on with fraying rope, Kendra Ullyart's design gave an overall impression of a theatre, built by the beggars themselves, which could collapse at any moment. Lighting by David Hersey.

performance. Most dramatic works are written in an episodic form with irregular jumps forward (or sometimes backwards) in time. These changes in time may be accompanied by changes in place, and the nature and extent of such time and place changes are a major component of visual style.

The stylistic options available to a stage environment are virtually unlimited, from a bare stage where the only statement comes from the pattern and texture of the floor boards to a complex setting so realistically constructed that it could almost be lived in, were it not for the open structuring to permit communication with an audience.

A pictorial or graphical representation may illustrate the details of an environment rather than provide its structure. Objects may be selected to identify the actor in a special place — or to stress its universality. Their significance may stem from isolated simplicity or be built up from juxtapositions. They may be symbolic or atmospheric. Or cynical. Or satirical. They may locate the action or comment

Designing Benjamin Britten's chamber opera *The Turn of the Screw* for the open space of Glasgow's Tramway, Vicki Mortimer set such simple elements as tarpaulin, water, ironwork and a window on an earth and bark floor. Lighting by Alan Burrett.

upon it. They may overstate or understate. They may place audience imagination under strict control or allow it free reign. Variations in time and place may vary from total changes to delicate hints. Between heightened naturalism and total symbolism there is an unlimited range of departures from reality. Which one will provide the best visual metaphor for the play and support the actors in their interpretation of it for the audience?

LIGHTING STYLE

Lighting often has to form a stylistic bridge between near naturalistic acting and the non-naturalism of the scenic environment. Light in a real life situation is generated naturally by sun, moon and stars, and artificially by lamps. But its quality is mostly the result of complex reflections from every surface in the environment. In a room lit by daylight, the light through the windows may include some direct rays from the sun. But a large component of the light (in many cases all of it) will be reflected light from the sky and from the surfaces of buildings outside the window. If we try to light a realistic stage room by placing a single large source outside the window, there will be light for the actors to see each other but it will have neither the quantity nor quality to help them to make contact with the audience. Naturalistic light can be simulated by making it appear to be

Only in an occasional modern work are the dancers able to interact with the setting to any significant extent: normally their movement requires so much clear space that settings must be banished to the back and sides of the stage space. But this is a challenge which designers continue to meet as in Lila di Nobili's designs for Frederick Ashton's *Ondine* for the Royal Ballet.

motivated by sources in the sky and by real light fittings which are either in view or presumed to be just out of sight. But as a back up to these obvious sources many spotlights are required to project the effect of reflected light in a sufficiently exaggerated way to help the actors project. For the audience to accept such lighting as realistic, it must appear to conform to the logic of natural light in terms of its direction, balance, colour, shadows, etc.

The need to provide sufficient light for such expressive acting resources as eyes and teeth to be clearly visible to an audience ensures that a considerable heightening of any attempt at near-naturalism is inevitable. Heightening will also arise from the need to light from angles which sculpt both actor and scene, to overcome the flattening which any three-dimensional staging is inevitably subjected to when viewed frontally from any but the smallest of auditoria.

While all lighting styles are likely to call for a sculptural illumination, there are other options which light can offer to a stage production. Light can be used selectively to help concentrate the audience attention on chosen areas of the stage action — light can be used to conceal as well as to reveal. And it can be used

Without the possibility of walls, theatre-in-the-round is dependent upon floor and furniture to suggest interior realism. For this production of J.B. Priestley's *Dangerous Corner*, designed by Cathy Ryan, levels shaped by curves and right angles reflect the themes of the play and suggest spatial relationships between the characters. Lighting by Paul Jones.

to help create atmosphere. Whether it does either, neither or both will be a strong component of style. As will the extent to which we choose to deploy it. Selective and atmospheric lights can be given a credible logic in terms of nature. Or they can be used as a non-realistic production device. Or heightened realism can be combined with non-realism by deploying light changes of both a conscious and subconscious nature.

Thus it is quite possible to maintain something of a logical credibility, albeit considerably heightened, in relation to the natural behaviour of light, yet use it as a dramatic tool in a visual style which is considerably removed from reality.

THE SEARCH FOR STYLE

Choice of an appropriate style is the key decision facing any production team, and the search for this style is the starting point in the preparation of a text and/or music score for performance. As noted, the extent to which the style departs from reality can vary in the acting, costume, setting and lighting — although each must be internally consistent and complementary to the others.

4 SPACE AND TIME

A key element in the designer's visual language is the means by which stage space can be manipulated within a time sequence. During any performance, whatever the style, there will certainly be a progression of time and this may possibly also involve changes of place. The various means of handling such changes are a major constituent of a designer's visual vocabulary. Like everything else that happens on a stage, the chosen method will both derive from, and contribute to, the overall production style.

While it is possible to leave to the actors' words the stimulation of all the appropriate changes in the audience's imagination, most production styles seek the support of lighting changes and/or physical movements. Lighting changes are often used without physical movement: that is, the set remains static throughout with all changes of time and, where appropriate, place indicated by light. On the other hand, physical movements can be used without the light appearing to change in either quantity or quality, although a subtle technical re-balance will normally be required to avoid shadows on and from repositioned scenery.

PHYSICAL MOVEMENTS

Physical movements can be used to change the stage environment by repositioning elements of scenery already present, and/or by replacing, removing or adding other elements. These changes may take place within sight of the audience or be hidden behind a curtain or other form of screening. The drawing of a curtain is a method now rarely used (unless as part of a very positive style, possibly with historic associations) since it breaks up the continuity of a play's development. However, some designs allow the action to continue in front of downstage scenery which masks a change taking place behind. Hidden changes may use virtually any technique, including assembly from many component parts: the only constraints are the time available and the need to proceed quietly. For moving sets in sight of an audience, whether they appear to move of their own accord or are positioned with the aid of actors, several methods are available.

Flying

Perhaps the simplest way of changing scenery is by lowering and raising it in a vertical plane between the stage and a storage area above. Such flying is so central to theatre technology that all mainstream theatres built during the last hundred years or so have been provided with this facility, despite the costs and other problems of a fly tower whose grid for pulleys needs to be at least two and a half times the proscenium height.

Most scenery is hoisted manually: while simple theatres follow the old tradition of using unassisted muscle, the usual method is to balance the load with a counterweight so that even the heaviest pieces can be flown smoothly by one person. Various powered systems have been devised but until very recently they lacked the timing finesse of the human hand.

For a designer, the frustration of flying is the need for all pieces to fly in the same plane. While it is relatively simple to fly a single piece at an angle, and possible to fly two or three others at different angles provided their paths do not cross, there are severe limitations on the extent to which this can be done. To fly even one piece at an angle which is not parallel to the rest requires careful planning involving not just the scenery but all the static elements suspended from the grid such as masking and lighting. It can be done, especially in a production which uses minimal flying, but in general flying has to be regarded as something that takes place in a plane parallel to the front of the stage. Although this is undoubtedly a restriction, flying used with other movement techniques, and perhaps with perspective exaggerations in the construction or painting, can contribute to an illusion of complex spatial movement.

Sinking

For scenic movements in a vertical plane, the obvious alternative to flying them above the stage is to sink them below. Most Victorian stages were equipped to do this to a greater or lesser degree. The most common traps were the corner traps, downstage left and right, intended not for scenery but for instant appearance of actors. (When fitted with a series of hinged segments in the shape of a star — the star trap — an actor could be, and in Christmas pantomime still is, shot magically through the stage floor.) More upstage and central there was usually a rectangular grave trap inspired by *Hamlet*. Trapping of this kind is still used today for such moments as Papageno's food and drink in *The Magic Flute*, but the tendency is to construct new stage floors in a modular way which allows traps to be positioned anywhere required by the designer.

Many Victorian stages had a complex structure comprising a series of elevators (known as bridges) which could sink below or rise above stage level, carrying scenery or actors. Between each bridge was a slot through which two-dimensional scenery could be positioned. Today's equivalent is the highly mechanised stages of the central European opera houses, where the stage is divided into a series of elevators which can bring entire scenes from the basement or be used to form a series of levels, and in some cases be tilted to form an inclined stage to the designer's designated rake. Such stages are intended mainly for handling the twice daily changeovers, in repertoire theatres, between rehearsals and an evening programme which rotates several productions.

Permanent installations of bridges and traps, even the most sophisticated (or one might even say, particularly the most sophisticated) rarely offer their facilities in exactly the right place for a particular production design. It is the trappable stage that offers fullest flexibility — provided that the theatre is operating longish runs.

Thus, whereas flying in mainstream theatres is normal practice with a considerable degree of standardisation, sinking is either a matter of adapting to an existing specialised installation or including the necessary engineering in the design. The answer to a designer's question 'Can we fly?' is normally a straightforward yes or no, whereas the question 'Can we sink?' is likely to start a debate which reveals so many problems that a simpler solution is sought.

Sliding

Flying scenery usually has to be designed as flat as possible: either two-dimensional cloths or three-dimensional structures with minimum depth. This restriction is purely to conserve space for other flying scenery and for suspending lighting equipment. If changes of large chunks are to be made, it is normal to push them on from the side, although such lateral movements may also be used for flat pieces if desired. The juxtaposition of vertical and lateral movements can make for a particularly satisfying visual experience if the timing is right.

The use of painted flats at the sides of the stage is theatre's longest running scenographic tradition. Standard practice from the earliest indoor theatres and throughout the eighteenth and nineteenth centuries, the technique is still used extensively in dance because it leaves a large area of the stage clear and provides multiple entrances.

Georgian and Victorian stages used elaborate mechanisms to replace one set of wings by another by sliding all the wings at exactly the same moment. With borders replaced in a simultaneous crossfly, this had a magic which can still be experienced at Drottningholm Court Theatre (near Stockholm), using the original designs and machinery. Eighteenth century sliders were fixed to the floor, but when flats or curtains are to be slid into position today, they are normally suspended from a track.

The standard tracks used for curtain movements are tab-tracks and wipes. A *tab-track* provides the traditional movement of paired curtains meeting at, and parting from, a centre point where the two sections of track overlap to provide a positive closure. A *wipe* is a single track which allows a single curtain to travel the full stage width if desired. Tracks may be motorised, hand winched, or have a line pulled hand-over-hand. As with most things in theatre, hand operation can allow more sensitive timing if the weight load permits. Wiping a single curtain, or wiping paired curtains with an asymmetric overlap, can provide a much more interesting revelation to a new scene than conventional centre opening tabs. And scenic elements, singly or in series, arriving or departing on tracks can be a powerful image — either as a purely visual happening between scenes or integrated with the text.

Trucks

When three-dimensional elements of scenery have to be moved in sight they are mounted on castored trucks. These trucks are also used for speed and convenience in positioning scenery during non-visual changes. Trucks can be in any appropriate size or shape, but considerable thought needs to be given to the practicalities of their movements. If they are to be moved in sight, they can be designed in such a way that operators are masked while working behind. Positional stability can be provided by wedges between truck and floor or, better, by drop bolts connecting with holes in the floor. This method also ensures that the truck is in its correct position. However, holes in the stage can be unacceptable to the actors and various specialised castors and braking devices are available.

If actor movements permit, slender tracks may be fixed to the stage or included within the specially designed stage floor that has become a feature of so much contemporary design. In big shows, particularly musicals, the trucks are moved by winched steel cables running in the narrow void between the stage and the production's false floor — rather in the manner of cable cars. And trucks which remain on stage, but can be repositioned, have been successfully designed to move about a pivotal point fixed to the floor.

But perhaps the newest device with the most exciting potential is the *air castor* which enables trucks to be moved about the stage on an air cushion. When the air pressure is switched off, the truck settles very firmly on the floor, anchored by its own weight. Early air castors were very sensitive to irregularities and gaps in the floor, but new models are being developed with much greater tolerance.

Machinery

Machinery may be part of the permanent facilities of a stage or it can be devised and installed for a particular production. Permanent installations are too inflexible to be of much positive use to a designer. Although such equipment may occasionally coincide with the production's dynamic requirements, its intended use is more to shift massive opera sets between acts and to facilitate changes in repertoire. Many repertoire opera houses, therefore, have a series of wagon stages, each the size of the main acting area. On these, or on their modular sections, large sets can be manipulated in conjunction with the elevators discussed earlier.

Special machinery can be installed for long run big budget productions. In Las Vegas the girls descend in cages from the auditorium ceiling, walkways advance and retract, and the *Titanic* sinks twice nightly. In London's West End, hydraulics allow endless magic configurations on tight stages with negligible wing space. If a designer can demonstrate in model form exactly what should happen, machinery specialists can devise a solution at a price (the hole under the Piccadilly Theatre's stage foundations for the hydraulics for *Mutiny* is said to have cost £40,000 for excavations alone at 1985 prices).

On one point most designers are absolutely clear: away from the special problems of repertoire, it is better to have a clear trappable stage with generous wing space than a hi-tech mechanised stage which cannot hope to foresee future developments in production style.

Stage depth

There are two depth dimensions in a stage setting. The depth, structural or painted, of an individual piece of scenery. And the spatial depth determined by the relationships of the various pieces. It is the juxtaposition of scenic pieces that produces much of the designer's control of space, and so the difficulties of moving in diagonal planes are not quite the major restriction which they seem. Remarkably fluid progressions of stage space can be achieved with lateral and vertical movements in a series of planes parallel to the front of the stage. And such movements are relatively easy to control smoothly without their mechanical means being too obvious.

A major problem with changes in view is getting furniture on and off. Devices such as treadmills have been used in the downstage areas of musicals but are very limited in straight drama. When trucks are used they allow the scene to arrive with its furniture in position. But trucks are not always appropriate to a chosen production style. Moreover, while they can often contribute to elegant stage movements, it can be difficult to avoid clumsiness when getting them on and off stage via the wing masking.

LIGHTING CHANGES

To change the stage environment 'before your very eyes' is one of the most powerful techniques available to theatre. And this fluidity has been considerably enhanced by the developing possibilities of lighting.

Whether used on a static scene or in conjunction with physical movements, lighting variations can indicate progressions in time and shifts in place. Light can be used selectively and it can be used atmospherically: whether it is used for either, neither or both in a production is a matter of production style.

Selective light changes

Light can be thought of as concealing as well as revealing, providing that the ability to conceal is not taken too literally. Selective lighting depends upon emphasis of what we wish to select in contrast to that which we do not. It is rarely possible for unlit parts of the stage to go into total blackness because of the inevitable presence of reflected light. Indeed this reflected light can have such a random effect that it is often necessary to add some positive light of a different quality to the reflected light to dress areas of the stage which have not been positively selected with light. Furthermore, because lighting for the actor needs to come from a frontal angle if it is to make eyes and lips visible, the area of lit stage floor will not correspond exactly with the area in which the actors can be clearly seen.

Therefore the extent to which selective lighting is to be used as a production dynamic is a matter to be kept constantly in mind during the design process. It forms an important part of the debate between scene and lighting designers and with the director.

Atmospheric light changes

Lighting can contribute to the atmosphere of a scene and support the actors in their communication of shifting emotions during the unfolding of the drama. For example, quite delicate shifts of warm and cool can support a scene's development on a happy-sad axis, and varying contrasts of light and shade can help to underscore feelings of menace.

Whether the lighting will be used to support the progress of the natural day in respect of its sun and moon sources is a major matter for production style. In a play, since the roots of most acting lie in naturalism, the lighting will usually need at least to stem from nature — but with a very considerable departure being possible, provided that a consistent relationship with both scenic and acting styles is maintained.

However, with careful planning, it is possible for light to relate to nature, yet contribute to shifts in both selectivity and atmosphere.

The fluidity of lighting can progress with two different dynamics, if necessary simultaneously, within the same production. Light can change instantly or over any chosen period of time — and at a variable rate within that chosen overall time span. The audience will be consciously aware of the faster changes but will only perceive the slower ones subconsciously. Conscious light changes are a powerful tool for indicating progressions in time and place. Subconscious changes also help to progress the dramatic action in this way, but they have an even stronger potential to support, perhaps through the subtlest variations in colour, the delicate flow of emotions.

The use of conscious and subconscious (either, neither or both) light changes, whether for selection or atmosphere (either, neither or both) are strong components of production style. Choice of an appropriate mix is a matter for the production team: productions in the philosophic tradition of Brecht are unlikely to use subconscious variations in subtle tints but will seek a strong, balanced but constant light, tinted with the palest steels and greys to enhance the light's cold clear clarity. (Brecht's light was rarely unfiltered white: he added a touch of blue to give whiter than white in the manner of detergent manufacturers.)

Sculptural lighting

Whereas selectivity and atmosphere are optional contributions, light has a sculptural role in every production. The larger the auditorium, the more the stage becomes distanced from the audience and there is a tendency, increased by the framing effect of the proscenium arch, for the performers and their environment to become flattened. Directional light can not only reveal three-dimensional form but enhance it to compensate for the flattening effect of distant viewing. Light has a threefold sculpting role:

* To sculpt the performer, particularly the actor's face and the dancer's body to ensure that they do not become two-dimensional cut-outs when viewed from afar.

* To reveal the three-dimensional quality of individual scenic elements and the spatial relationships between them.

* To separate the performers from the structure of their environment, increasing apparent stage depth and ensuring that they do not merge with the scenic background.

Visibility

The major problem in realising a lighting design concept is to preserve sufficient facial visibility for the actor to communicate, while exploiting light's ability to sculpt, select and create atmosphere. The difficulties associated with selecting an area of the stage floor while endeavouring to light an actor's face (especially those major means of an actor's projection, the eyes and teeth) have already been mentioned. Considering that both sculpting and atmosphere imply light and shade — i.e. absence of light — it may be noted that the most potentially powerful uses of light in a theatre designer's visual vocabulary are at war with light's most essential contribution to life — visibility.

PROJECTION

The optical projection of images forms a powerful part of the designer's visual vocabulary. Indeed, with rather monotonous regularity, projection has been proposed (often with an eye to financial economies) as an alternative to a constructed scenic environment. 'Doing it all with lighting' is another proposal that pops up on a regular basis. However, both with lights and projection it is the surface on which the light or image falls that is the key to the visual statement. And projection is certainly not a cheap alternative: apart from equipment and materials, projection needs one of theatre's most expensive commodities — time.

Projection techniques span the production of the simplest static textures through to the fluid manipulation of complex detailed images. Available methods include:

Gobos

The simplest form of projection is the gobo, a two-dimensional outline mask whose shape can be projected by any spotlight which has profile optics (and those are now the most common form of spotlight). Gobo masks are cut in thin alloy which will withstand the intense heat at the optical centre of the instrument (the 'gate') where they have to be positioned. Gobos can vary from very simple break-up patterns for texture to very complex images. An ever-increasing library of stock images is available but virtually any image can be produced to order from a designer's artwork by specialist manufacturers using a lithographic process.

However, simple texturing of the light is possibly the most interesting application of a gobo — whether in an almost naturalistic way, such as an impression of dappled light falling through trees, or a means of gently softening a light when it might otherwise fall too harshly on a scene. The texture can be built up through superimpositions, when it gains from different degrees of softness/hardness in the focus. Textured light falling on textured material is visually interesting, as are scenery and actors moving in textured light. Rotating discs are available to put an illusion of movement into the gobo and this is particularly useful for producing such effects as shimmering.

Scenic projection

For many years the major technical problem of scenic projection was intensity. A good bright image could be produced on an otherwise blacked-out stage but when light was added for the actors, the projection image faded by comparison. If the direction of the light beams was carefully planned to avoid the screen, and the set (especially the stage floor) kept as near black as possible, good images were possible provided the acting area was distanced as much as possible from the images. Alas, the resultant impression of gloom was hardly supportive of many scripts. However, more powerful projectors are now available. These are particularly bulky because, apart from their complex condenser optics and the fans required to protect slides and lenses, the special discharge lamps cannot be dimmed electrically and so the image has to be faded mechanically by motorised shutters.

These projectors use a large slide (18cm × 18cm; 7in × 7in) which can be either painted by the designer or prepared photographically. Projection from an angle other than flat-on has to be compensated for by a calculated distortion of the image on the slide.

To cover such large areas as cycloramas, big opera houses often mount pairs of these projectors high up on the lighting towers immediately upstage of either side

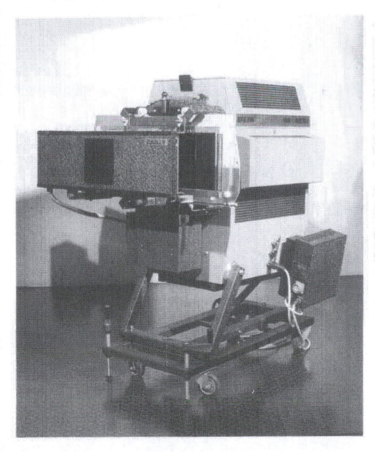

The *Pani BP 4* is the international standard instrument for high intensity scenic projection in large theatres and opera houses. The light source is a 4kW HMI discharge lamp and slides are 18cm × 18cm (7in × 7in). The Austrian firm of Ludwig Pani have also developed this even more powerful 6kW projector using 24cm × 24cm (9½in × 9½in) slides.

Annelies Corrodi, designer of *The Flying Dutchman* at Zurich Opera, used 14 Pani projectors for a sequence of dissolving images which included the setting of sails by superimposition and the gradual transformation of the ship to a skeletal hulk.

The Dutchman's ship.

Fate superimposed.

The ship has disappeared, leaving a brooding seascape.

In *Their Day*, Svoboda used projected images on multiple screens to focus upon specific elements in an environment and alter their scales.

of the proscenium arch. Each projector lights across to the other side of the stage so that the picture is formed by a pair from each side. Image dissolving is then possible by crossfading between pairs, with the tower access allowing manual changing of slides between crossfades. This ability to cut or dissolve images for a fast fluidity of location is a major reason for choosing projection. Another reason is that it produces the kind of luminous quality that can be an appropriate style for particular stage works.

However, this will be dependent upon the surface on which the image falls. Simple screens are rarely appropriate because they look like what they are: screens, and this is only likely to be acceptable under very positive circumstances. Black screen material is available, with optional grades for accepting an image from the front or from the rear. Their slight plasticy sheen can be disguised by the addition of a black scrim. But projection can also go on to most types of surface: how textured this surface can be will depend upon the nature of the image and the effect desired. Screens have been made from many parallel strings and even from rubber strips to allow actors to burst through the image. Or surfaces with many openings on which, for example, windows and doors can be projected, and then opened. The only limitations are imagination and budget.

Costume for *La Bête* by David Hirson at Citadel Theatre, Edmonton, Canada, designed by Ann Curtis. The play, although taking place in 1654, uses language and syntax so unmistakably modern that the production was set in 1994 with the company of classical actors in modern dress. Exceptions were seventeenth-century-type clothes worn by Valère, the vulgar street busker and Dorine, the stage-struck servant dressed in theatrical finery borrowed from the company's wardrobe.

COSTUME

Costume changes will help to indicate the length of a jump in time. Indeed many members of the audience will respond so perceptively to this that any mistakes will be immediately noticed. Lengthy time differences may require a change of clothes of different cut, but most will be shorter intervals and require a more subtle response. Clothes will be expected to mirror a character's ageing, and other factors include time of day, season of year and weather. And even if the conditions remain stable, the audience are well aware that clothes have a limited life.

Of these various methods of progressing time and place, several are likely to be appropriate to a particular production style. As always with style, it is consistency and integration that bring credibility.

5 SOME PRACTICALITIES

Most of life's ideals have to be tempered by practical realities and the theatre is no exception. Theatre designers are under constant pressure to focus their art rather more towards a pursuit of the possible than the desirable. This is difficult to equate with the relentless search for ideals that is fundamental to any art. However, the reality is that the carefully considered application of a little pragmatism can often enable a much closer realisation of an ideal to be achieved than would be possible with a more uncompromising approach.

Therefore, before discussing the process of designing a production, it is appropriate to consider some of the practicalities that a designer has to keep in mind.

BUDGETS

Money is obviously a major constraint. Indeed, lack of it is usually the prime problem when endeavouring to convert ideas into reality. Although it is inevitable that budgetary decisions are involved in the design process, it is important that they influence rather than inhibit. Excessive preoccupation with detailed costings during the early conceptual phases can distract from the fundamental process of exploring ideas. However, as a design develops, the designer increasingly has to establish priorities in an endeavour to remain within budgetary limitations. This requires making judgements based on cost-effectiveness. But how does one decide the relative effectiveness of the various alternatives and assess how much each will cost?

Experience provides a designer with something of an intuitive feel for basic costing, certainly enough to know whether major aspects of the design are generally proceeding within the budgeted price band. When a design seems to be developing in an apparently expensive way, advice sought after establishing the general format but before physical details are finalised will often suggest relatively minor modifications which are visually acceptable but offer considerable savings in construction costs. Support from a good production manager is the key to success in such costing exercises.

Cost is fact. Effectiveness however is a complex judgement which, although it can be based to some extent on a logic with which the rest of the production team can help, is mainly dependent upon the designer's aesthetic sensitivity as an artist. The designer can be under considerable pressure in making such decisions because there may be a temptation to spend on whichever alternative provides the most obvious visual return for money, rather than concentrate on support for the play and its players.

Budgeting is divided into two sectors: production costs and running costs. Although these are clearly defined areas, they interact in a way which is particularly influenced by the design. *Physical production* is the term generally used for the costs involved in preparing sets, costumes and props. This is obviously the area which forms the core of a design budget. However, the nature of the design will also have a knock-on effect on the running costs, particularly in the number of staff required to operate scene and lighting changes and to assist costume changes. Elaborate scene changes may call for extra performance staff. On the other hand introduction of mechanisation may increase production costs but reduce running staff numbers. The equation is a complex one, with the prospective length of the run a major factor, and requires close co-operation between production manager and design team.

There is very rarely enough openness about budgeting in the theatre world. The total budget and its subdivision into allocations for specific areas of expenditure are usually kept secret. Individuals have to be given a figure for their own area of responsibility, but all too frequently this figure is a rather hazy approximation, artificially reduced in a spirit of mistrust and optimism. Standard theatre management practice is only slowly beginning to discover, and consequently to recognise, the value of involving production team members in the budgeting process. Open debate about proportioning available money can be a particularly positive way of improving the effectiveness with which it is spent.

SCHEDULES

There are some things which money may not always be able to buy: particularly time. The many demands, most of them conflicting, made upon the use of the stage during the technical and dress rehearsal period require integration through careful scheduling. And scheduling, like budgeting, is an area where agreement rather than imposition is crucial to achieving the positive benefits which stem from a spirit of group involvement.

Creative processes are difficult to schedule. Even the most methodical approach to design involves decisions which are not logically based. It is not easy to timetable the arrival of an idea, particularly as many ideas are the result of an experimental process. During the early phases of preparation for a stage production, time is relatively flexible. Actors in the rehearsal room can probe and discard. Authors can rewrite. Designers can pursue visual ideas in model form. But with each day of the countdown to first performance, the need to take decisions increases. And many design decisions are irreversible, since they result in instructions to workshops involving the commitment of vast resources of both money and time.

The pace accelerates, climaxing when the production takes possession of the stage. At this point the time scale for assembling the environment and integrating the costumed actors with it is normally, at best, barely adequate. There is rarely any significant time for experiment — little opportunity for adapting the environment or even for the actors to explore any new possibilities which suggest themselves during this major transition from rehearsal room mark-up (or possibly mock-up) of the scenery to the real thing. The exceptions to this time squeeze are few indeed.

The key is a schedule which ensures firstly that everything that can possibly be made ready away from the stage is included in the preparations prior to the get-in. And secondly that stage time is apportioned to allow each department to have an appropriate share, in the right sequence but overlapping where the nature of the work allows.

The pressures of time mean that designers can leave nothing to chance. If something can only be finalised through experiment, they need to have a fall back alternative clearly in mind. While they should have confidence that the design will work, they also must have a flexible approach which will allow them to respond to any fresh idea which presents itself either to them or to colleagues in the creative team.

SIGHTLINES

A problem which is related to theatre architecture (and therefore of particular consequence when touring) is the restricted area of stage which can be viewed from certain seats. These lines of sight may be impeded vertically and/or laterally.

Vertical sightlines

In theatres with high balconies, the view of the upstage areas from the topmost seats is likely to be cut-off by the top of the proscenium arch or by a border hung as part of the design. The extent of this cut-off can be determined with the aid of a section through the centreline of auditorium and stage. As seats get higher it is inevitable that much of the rear of the set disappears from view. Vertical elements in the design will become distorted and actors will tend to be seen against a background of floor. Restricted visibility of the set has to be regarded as inevitable but careful consideration needs to be given to how well the actors can be seen when they move upstage.

Any problems will be multiplied if the stage level is raised by platforms, steps and ramps. Actors passing through a non-view area are acceptable: it is longish sequences of important plot played invisibly upstage which present concern. On some occasions this may be inevitable. But it should be part of a design decision, taken knowingly rather than just happening by default. And the theatre management should be informed as far in advance as possible.

Lateral sightlines

Seats to the side of the auditorium may have an impeded view of their own side of the stage. Boxes and the side portions of the circles in horseshoe theatres are the obvious areas of potential difficulty, although even the ends of rows in the orchestra stalls can present problems. As discussed in Chapter 2, sightlines in

Richard Hudson based this design for *The Rake's Progress* on the eighteenth century convention of wings and borders changing in front of the audience, choosing sharp acid colours to make the changes as striking as possible. (Other designs for *The Rake's Progress* are on page 57.)

Economy, simplicity and boldness were Peter J. Davison's visual aims for *Saint Joan*. The concrete bunker — cold, impersonal and towering — became the metaphor for the male world of inflexible systems in which Joan speaks. Rain, water, blue sky and stars were revealed and cruelly shut off by heavy sliding panels. Costumes by Clare Mitchell. Lighting by Mark Henderson.

Beowulf at The Sugar Factory, Odense, Denmark. Designer: Claire Lyth. Lighting by Jens Klastrup.

general and lateral ones in particular have been a major concern in the development of theatre architecture. Current thinking increasingly accepts that close
contact between actors and a compact audience is more important than uniform
purity of sightline. The one-sided view of the stage from side seats is compensated for by lower pricing, and in such theatres it is incumbent upon the directing/
designing team not to place extended big scenes at the extreme sides — or at least
only to do it while being aware of the consequences. Once again, a drawing, this
time in plan, will assist in determining parameters.

Keeping key scenes clear of the back and sides of the stage is not the major
hardship that it might seem on first consideration. To communicate with their
audience, actors are helped by being placed in the more central downstage areas
radiating from the stage's 'point of command' where an actor can embrace the
attention of every member of the audience.

MASKING

While sightlines affect what we wish the audience to see, masking controls what
we would prefer to remain hidden. Until about the middle of the present century, it
was normal practice to conceal the technical areas above and at the sides of the
stage. Indeed any failure to do so was regarded as lack of competence. Today's
masking — especially above the stage — is a design option. Except within a very
positive production style, which makes a point of the comings and goings of the
actor being obvious, some degree of side masking is essential to allow actors and
technicians to stand by unobserved.

Some sets are self-masking in that scenic structures not only define the acting
area, but mask off sight of anything beyond. Other styles, particularly those where
the structural elements are placed in central isolation in the manner of an island,
require a masking surround. This may be designed to make a positive statement or
in a way which is neutral yet relates supportively in colour and texture to the set.
Or it may be neutrally black with the intention of being unobtrusive when light is
focused on the central scenic elements.

Side masking may be arranged as a series of traditional wings set parallel to the
front of the stage. Or it may be set up-and-downstage in the form of a box. Up-
and-down masking tends to provide more of a sense of enclosure and it can be
more visually pleasing. On the other hand, on-and-off masking provides more
possibilities for actor entrances and for side lighting.

In today's theatre the area above the set is frequently left open and unmasked,
with the top limits of vision defined by the lighting equipment almost in the
manner of a ceiling. This can be apt in a play where there are no vertical flying
movements and a flytower which is clear of everything except lights. However,
even in this situation, the designer may wish to control just how much is visible by
the discreet use of neutral (probably black) borders. When top masking forms a
decorative visual element, its positioning must be carefully planned, not only to
mask but to allow light beams to reach their intended target.

FIRE REGULATIONS

The use of any material on stage is controlled by fire prevention regulations. These are strictly enforced by the licensing authorities through fire brigade officers who have powers to withhold permission for a performance to take place unless scenery and props made from unsuitable material are removed from the stage. Each set — and, on tour, each theatre — is normally inspected by a fire prevention officer who may check fire resistance by applying a test flame to selected pieces.

Some materials are inherently fireproof and others may be made fire retardant with the aid of chemicals. Fire retardant treatment is generally acceptable for scenery positioned upstage of the fire curtain in a proscenium theatre. Anything on the audience side of that curtain — and therefore everything on an open stage — must be constructed of inherently fireproof materials. Apart from the considerable budgetary implications of this, designers need to seek early advice, through the production manager, if they are considering using any new or non-orthodox material.

SAFETY

Fire prevention is just one aspect of safety. A stage is potentially a very dangerous place where temporary structures move horizontally and vertically in conditions of abruptly changing visibility. The floor is liable to have snaking cables, various levels and even opening and closing holes. Safety is essentially dependent upon commonsense and vigilance. The licensing of a theatre building has always been subject to certain safety regulations, particularly of electrical wiring and the maintenance of clear escape routes. As health and safety in the workplace becomes an increasing cause for general concern, there is a possibility that stages may become subject to general regulations which would be inappropriate and restrictive. This will only be avoided if theatre people approach safety in a responsible way. While advance planning is generally very good with, for example, technicians and licensing authorities co-operating in the application of fail-safe devices to mechanised scenery, there are dangers in taking short cuts during rehearsals when people are tired yet anxious to beat the clock in a spirit of 'the show must go on'.

STABILITY

An aspect which is perhaps related rather more to actors' confidence in safety, rather than actual safety, is the stability of the scenery, particularly raised levels. Designers may understandably wish for a balcony which elegantly spans a pair of slender supporting columns. But if such a structure is to be moveable, it may not be possible to construct such a span free from an unnerving feeling of shakiness. If in doubt, the designer should talk to the workshops before taking detailed design too far.

MOVEMENT

But stability in its turn is just one aspect of the need for an environment in which actors can move confidently. Stairs without a handrail or even a balustrade, which might be quite acceptable in a house or garden, can become rather frightening to an actor confronted with the void of a theatre auditorium. Steep raked floors may lose some of their visual impact if actor confidence is impaired by problems of maintaining their balance or even just a foothold.

COSTUMES

But a set which allows freedom of movement is not enough: that freedom must be extended to the costumes. While many aspects of period cut will help an actor to behave in a period way, there is usually need for less rigidity than would be imposed by the total historical accuracy of real period clothes. And consideration needs to be given to the kind of specialist movement implied by such actions as dancing, singing or fencing.

And there have, alas, been productions with splendid visual co-ordination between sets and costumes — but doors with insufficient width for a costumed actor to pass through with dignity.

REPERTOIRE

The problems of repertoire have been touched on in earlier chapters. *Run* or *rep* is one of the great divides facing designers. A run may be for days, weeks or years (or even for ever, like Agatha Christie's *Mousetrap*) and the set and lighting can be designed to remain continuously in position. In repertoire, the shows may alternate as frequently as daily and the set is normally required to be erected and its lighting focused in half a day or less — and struck even quicker. All countries operate a mix of the systems, although Anglo-American theatre has mostly runs whereas that of central Europe is largely based on daily change.

TOURING

The second major division is resident or touring. While some productions play only in one theatre and can be specifically designed for that stage, many productions have to be sufficiently flexible to tour a sequence of different stages. When theatres had a standardised form, the width of the proscenium opening was the only variable of any real consequence to the designer. But today's tours are performed in venues of all kinds and it can be quite difficult to find any significant common denominators between the various stages to be visited.

When proscenium opening was the only constraint and the range of design styles was narrower, box sets were designed so that they could be 'opened out' to fill a larger opening by adjusting the angles at which the constituent flats joined each other. Apart from the visual distortion, the resultant changes to the acting area are unacceptable to the precisely choreographed movements of most current directing styles.

However, what happens when a set designed for a 9m (30ft) opening is placed on a stage with a 13m (42ft) width? (And some touring theatres are considerably wider.) Filling the gaps at the side with neutral masking tends to produce a heavy framing effect. And when that 9m (30ft) set is placed behind an 8m (26ft) opening, the lines of sight from seats at the auditorium side become unsatisfactory. The old practice of leaving out sections of the set is no longer acceptable if it affects the size and style of the acting area. However, non-functional pieces with only a visual function are sometimes temporarily discarded on a stage which lacks space.

Island setting is the style which probably lends itself most naturally to touring: the acting area is precisely defined by the floor, and the masking surround can be designed to allow for adjustment to a wide range of stage dimensions.

Many fringe theatre companies plan their productions with a flexibility to adapt to virtually any size, shape and mode of performing space. The more mainstream tours however are normally proscenium — or at least end-stage — oriented and designed for an optimum opening of about 8.5m (28ft).

Although width is perhaps the main concern, practical influences on design also include:

- *Depth*. What will happen on a particularly shallow stage? Can non-functional items be omitted without too much visual consequence? Or can the set be compressed without restricting the acting area?

- *Off-stage areas*. Space for manoeuvring is not only likely to be restricted but will vary on each stage between left, right and rear.

- *Transportability* implies a set that can be constructed to breakdown into sections which are as lightweight and pack as flat as possible. Yet everything, including the costumes, needs to be particularly ruggedly built to withstand handling much in excess of that normal in a resident theatre.

- *Size*. The total volume of the set, its complexity, and the dimensions of its individual pieces, are likely to be more constrained by budgets (trucking costs, crew size for getting in and out) and schedules (available fit-up time) than would be the case for a run in a single theatre.

One night stands

The traditional standard tour stop is for a week or multiple of a week. However, part weeks or one nights have become increasingly common, particularly at each end of the touring spectrum — the small alternative plays and the major musicals. One, two and three night stands tend to play non-conventional venues and therefore offer designers the compounded challenge of flexibility and speed, coupled with a non-apparent simplicity.

Lighting on tour

Lighting is constrained by the installation in each theatre, particularly the location of spotlight positions in the auditorium, and by the time available for rigging, focusing and plotting. On a production with complex lighting, the cost of touring the entire on-stage lighting rig complete with its own pre-memorised control desk may be justified by time savings. However, the effectiveness of a touring lighting design will always be primarily dependent on the designer giving full consideration to set-up time available in each venue and to the differing lighting angles that each auditorium will offer.

All these problems are compounded for the design team because the full list of touring dates is frequently incomplete at the time of the design process.

6 THE DESIGN PROCESS

Theatre designing involves alternating periods of working in isolation and as a member of a group. This can be quite stressful and coping requires a theatre designer to have, or develop, a rather special temperament. Creative work carried out in isolation is very personal and a designer becomes very possessive of the results. It can therefore be quite difficult to share work-in-progress by submitting it for group discussion.

Showing an unfinished design stimulates objective comment from those who have not shared the creative agonies and possibly have a less acute visual sensitivity. But they are deeply involved, through the expertise of their own special areas, in the process of lifting the drama from the page. A process which is dependent upon interaction between all contributing creative skills.

There are agonies for writers in the first handing over of a script, and for actors in the first revealing of a tentative undeveloped performance. But from that moment they tend to be involved almost continuously in a group experience whereas designers have to keep returning to the isolation of the studio to develop their work. During this the designs will emerge from time to time for a sequence of group considerations involving various combinations of director, author, producer, lighting designer, production manager, actors, stage managers, cutters, carpenters and composers, all seeking the modifications that are desirable from their own particular viewpoint.

Throughout the production process a designer's work comes under continual scrutiny from colleagues, just as their contributions are scrutinised by the designer. During this it is very important for everyone to remember that comment is only really helpful if it is positive about perceived strengths as well as weaknesses.

There is no single standard method of progressing a design from first idea to first night. Each designer develops their own personal working approach. What is offered here is a possible process for those unsure how to proceed or those seeking an insight into the problems facing the designer. While the method for reaching decisions may vary, the problems remain reasonably constant as does the sequence in which they need to be tackled.

SCRIPT STUDY

Anyone working on a play begins with a study of the script: an initial straight read-through followed by a series of increasingly detailed analyses, preferably punctuated by further straight reads to keep the details in context. Few people find script reading easy. Which is hardly surprising since dialogue is intended to be heard rather than read. However, there is an advantage in the first contact being through eye rather than ear: a speaker will inevitably impose a personal interpretation whereas a reader can more readily keep an open and exploratory mind.

Occasionally, a designer may work in a situation where the design can develop in parallel with rehearsals. The script may not exist, but even if it does the designer might elect not to read it prior to sharing the rehearsal process with the actors in order to let their developing characters stimulate the appropriate clothes and environment. However, normal theatre organisation very rarely provides sufficient time for this approach so that many decisions have already been taken by the time of the first rehearsal, and much of the design work not only completed but construction underway.

So, in a normal situation, the starting point is for the designer to have an initial encounter with the script, letting it stimulate some ideas of who the people are and the possible environments they might inhabit. This is likely to take the form of mixed behavioural and visual images, and any transfer from mind to paper may well take the form of fragmentary sketches, rarely realistic, and accompanied by verbal notes which are probably in question form.

INITIAL DISCUSSIONS

At this point the designer is sufficiently familiar with the script to start probing it in discussion with the director. It is likely that the director will have been working longer on the text than the designer and may bring quite strong views on production style to this first session. However, a director's initial concern for style is likely to be focused on a verbal interpretation of the text, with thoughts on the visual aspects limited to a few general adjectives like minimal, pictorial, representational or symbolic. Some directors may offer the name of a painter who seems appropriate to their vision of the play, and words like Fragonard and Magritte can be useful triggers for a designer's research (or dreadful warnings!). However, director thinking at this point is more likely to be in terms of production mechanics, particularly the need for solutions to the staging of difficult moments.

Although there are notable exceptions, it is surprising just how few directors are visual thinkers; although many, but by no means all, can respond to a visual idea when shown it. These are the directors with whom a designer can have the most positive creative relationships — satisfying for both of them and for the interpretation of the play.

The result of this initial discussion will hopefully be a tentative agreement on the areas to be explored for how the piece might be staged. The designer should now have some awareness of how complex the director finds the subtext of the play. Whether any aspects, obvious or implied, such as political undertones, historical parallels or particular character relationships are likely to be stressed. There will have been some discussion on the general environment but this is more

(Left) The drawing of Papageno in the first printed edition of the libretto of *The Magic Flute* is an invaluable reference for any designer who wishes to get close to Mozart's intent. (Right) In 1978 David Hockney paid homage to the original but transformed it into an image which is both universal and of today.

likely to have been in philosophic or even doctrinaire terms. (Brecht's name will almost certainly have been mentioned!) Major potential staging problems will have been identified.

Within this framework the designer can now embark upon a more detailed study of the text and a search for visual imagery. The text work is in one sense the easier of the two. Although a hard slog, it requires logical analysis rather than having and sifting ideas. It involves a lot of breaking down, particularly into an events sequence of the drama's progress through place and time. (The old theatre term 'running order' is useful here.) It can be helpful to make lists. Lists of costumes and changes required by each character. Lists of apparently unavoidable moments when people interact with setting or props in a very specific way.

MUSIC STUDY

If the project is a piece of music theatre, initial study will include the score. Opera study will be based on the music. Very few designers have sufficient score reading ability to enable them to hear a new work by reading its notes on the page. However, most standard opera and musicals are now commercially recorded, and indeed it is often the appearance of a recording that stimulates the revival of operas which have been neglected for a century or more. New works, except for rock-based musicals, are rarely recorded in orchestral form prior to their first production, but piano tapes are usually available. Whether made to encourage investors to fund a musical or to assist vocal coaches with the composer's tempi and phrasing indications in a new opera, these tapes are invaluable aids to the production team. Familiarity with the composer's style from recordings of earlier works can help foster an image of the orchestrated sound. Playing the music initially as background is a help in absorbing its style. When familiar, it can be listened to with concentration while following the words and notes in the score. And during detailed work on the design, it can provide considerable inspirational help as background.

THE SEARCH FOR A STYLE

Style decisions, first general and then increasingly detailed, are at the heart of the design process. A dramatic text or music score may be realised for performance in many alternative styles and the initial approach of director and designer should be as open and exploratory as possible. Once the style has been agreed, they have to be convinced that the chosen way is the only one and they should be able to transmit this conviction to all with whom they work including, eventually, the audience. After the production is over, everyone can revert to an objectivity which admits that there are other styles in which the piece could have been performed just as successfully (or at least almost as successfully!).

A major problem for director and designer is the pressure they feel to be original. The more a piece has been performed the more they feel a need to find a fresh way of interpretation. With major classics the results of this can sometimes seem close to gimmickry, with details of character and even plot being subjected to considerable distortion in order to fit a concept. A new play is relieved of such pressures — if it seems to need only a chair, then it can be given only that chair.

Whereas subsequent productions may exploit one particular aspect of the piece at the expense of other aspects, the first production tends to seek a balanced interpretation of the whole. A particular feature of great classics is that they are multi-faceted. To reveal everything about each one during the course of a single production can be virtually impossible. But different productions can focus on different aspects of the characters or underlying philosophies. Success implies revealing depths without introducing distortions.

The search has to begin with the words and, if appropriate, the music. For the director they will tend to trigger ideas of human behaviour patterns, personal interactions and philosophies; and will be considered within the general context of a verbal debate. The designer's response to the same words and music will be more visual. People will be characterised not so much by what they say and how they say it, but by the way that their behaviour manifests itself in their appearance, particularly the clothes they wear, and in the objects they choose and the environment they inhabit.

Such differences in response between different members of the team are not clear-cut but overlapping, and during the search for style the sharing of viewpoints should feed each other's developing understanding of the piece.

Writers and composers

On a play's first production, its author will be available to help with questions of interpretation and to clarify ambiguity by rewriting as necessary. However, such a resource is rarely available to subsequent productions. Absence of a composer from the debate is much less critical than that of a playwright. Music notation is rather more precise than scripted dialogue and scope for interpretation is confined to nuances within a quite rigid framework.

Playwrights and composers are rarely able to offer a detailed visualisation of the people they have created in words and music — or the world they inhabit. Indeed, writers need and welcome a designer's creative collaboration in developing the visual aspects. And while they might not recognise when the designer has got it nearly right, they will almost certainly know when it is absolutely right.

Background research

Having acquired not just a growing knowledge but an understanding of the script, the designer is ready for a research phase. It may be appropriate to study background material. Perhaps the play has been adapted from a novel. The play (or the original novel) may be part of a sequence where the characters can be found developing before and after. It could have been adapted from another medium — may already have been a film or video. An opera libretto might have been adapted from a play. Analytical studies may have been published.

Studying such material can be useful, but there is an element of danger. It should only be seen as background information which may help the production team to understand the text. Everything that happens on stage should seem to stem from the text itself.

Performance research

Old plays are very seldom performed in the staging style of their first performances. Indeed, when seeking a style, this is likely to be the only one rejected immediately and completely. Most revivals are approached as plays for today, seeking to emphasise their relevance for a contemporary audience. Even when a play is revived in a period style, the attempt is to convey the manners of life in that period rather than the way they were portrayed on the stage.

However, there are currently some signs that we shall soon see more productions in the style of their original performances. The stimulus is coming from the opera world where there are simultaneous movements to find contemporary relevance in the standard repertoire and to attempt the spirit of the performances of the composer's time. The rediscovery of original instruments has made enormous strides over the past decade. With the aid of research by musicologists, players have studied baroque and classical bowing on gut strings and have remastered the old keyless wind instruments. With singers phrasing in period manner, we are again hearing the sounds of the eighteenth century and early nineteenth century in their original form rather than through a romantic gloss.

This sound is being heard increasingly in the opera house in conjunction with modern production styles. However, research into early acting, movement and staging is opening up the possibility of historical accuracy in performance. This is worlds apart from the stock gestures and painted landscapes that have so often made opera seem a moribund form to those nurtured in the playhouse. So, with a considerable number of theatres around the world being restored to the original condition in which they housed these works when new, it becomes possible to recreate the spirit of the original performances. The historical restoration can never be total because we can only see the past through the eyes of our own generation. Nevertheless, there is a whole new potential area of suspension of disbelief here — original sounds and sights catalysed by candle, oil or gaslit ambience. A few such productions would surely not only prove interesting as free-standing experiences but would enhance our insight into the works for performing them in today's styles — *to move forward first look back.*

Visual research

However, the key research for a designer is the hunt for visual images. Starting points are triggered by the text in two main areas: historical and geographical. In both the search is likely to have a sociological focus. The visual characteristics of social groupings of people in the context of places and period. Clothes worn, objects used, the natural environment and their modification of it.

The principal resources are libraries, museums and observation of the life around us. Books are perhaps the best starting point. They allow initial searching to be speedy and wide ranging. There is much to be said for research not being too specific at the beginning. Within certain loose target areas it can have a considerable random element, leafing through pages for the images that arrest the eye. At this point bibliographies, catalogues and indices are probably less use than open access to the stacks of a good library of picture books, shelved clearly by subject, and including bound volumes of magazines, Sunday supplements, cuttings, etc. Indexing comes into its own at a later phase when ideas begin to develop and the trail becomes more specific. With growth of computer cataloguing, the retrieval of information about where to find an image will become increasingly easy. Indeed, we can anticipate a time when vast collections of actual images will be stored in computer for instant retrieval and examination. But picture quality on a video screen may limit the usefulness of computers to the initial search for images. Not only may a video picture lack some of the finer detailing of the original but the image has a translucency which makes it differ considerably from that drawn or printed on paper. The image which a designer wishes to study in detail is likely to be the more tangible one on paper.

And even a printed image will only be a substitute for the real painting, photograph or object. Which takes the trail to museums. Here, as in the library, the options are to study the reality of the object, the selective reality of the photograph or the subjective reality of the painting.

(Above) Osbert Lancaster and (below) David Hockney both took engraver's line techniques as a starting point for designing Stravinsky's *The Rake's Progress*.

Discarding

The initial research phase presents an opportunity to exercise a key design skill: the ability — and the will — to reject one's own cherished ideas. Discarding is an action that naturally becomes more and more difficult as a design proceeds. In the later stages of model making it can mean abandoning the results of many hours of labour. But such work is rarely wasted: it is part of the necessary experimental process of developing an idea and testing it against its relevance to the words and music. The restart is almost always from a point of much greater understanding.

Who are the people?

Design work often starts with the set. There can be some pressure for this from the director. Not so much conscious pressure perhaps, but a director's natural wish to get on with thinking through the mechanics of staging. However, there is much in favour of starting with the costume designs. Who are the people? What are their beliefs, aspirations and interactions? Even if the writing is concerned with the deepest of moral and philosophical concepts, its probing of these will be through the human mind and will be concerned with its effects on the human condition.

So, who are the people? What do their clothes tell us about them as individuals? About their status in their society? About period? About place? This may not be the moment for final costume designs but initial sketches will establish the people, and help confirm agreement between writer, director and designer. In some circumstances these sketches might promote a useful debate with the actors — or perhaps assist the casting.

(Opposite) Ita Maximowna's first sketch designs for *Fidelio* underwent a considerable development process, but the essential concept was carried through to performance (above). (Gunther Rennert's production at Glyndebourne, lighting by Francis Reid.)

People influence the world around them. Their environment is a mixture of circumstance and their adaptation of it and to it. Therefore much of a stage setting can flow from a consideration of the characters. A clear visualisation of the people can trigger much of the spatial structuring and visual aesthetic of the stage settings.

But people and place interact and, whichever we start with, set and costume ideas will feed each other and full development of both will proceed in parallel.

DESIGN MEDIA

Costume designs are presented in the form of drawings but a three-dimensional scale model is the normal core of a completed set design. This may be supported with drawings in the form of a storyboard sequence to show the way in which the model will be used. And eventually there will also be plans and sections to define its dimensions precisely. However, in earlier phases of the set design process, drawings tend to be mainly an aid to tentative explorations, or a means of visual communication in the debate with the rest of the production team.

Sketch models

Normal model scale is 1:25. It is a scale which most theatre people's eyes are accustomed to reading and it produces a model which is reasonably transportable. (At this scale most designs, except for the big opera houses, will go through the door of a London taxi.) Initial modelling however is sometimes at the smaller scale of 1 : 50 or even 1 : 100 and this enables and encourages rapid and economic experimenting, proportioning and rejecting. Such early models are known as sketch models and, in addition to their value in working through ideas, a series of them can be used as a discussion aid in proposing alternative approaches or demonstrating a time sequence.

The model

Most of the work up to this point is in the nature of preliminary exploration. For most designers, the decisive creative work is done in the 1 : 25 model. The model provides a means of developing an aesthetic visual response and testing the validity of that response against the various specific needs of the play. Consequently the model is something of an art form in its own right, although its essential function is as the centrepiece of communication between the designer and everyone concerned with the production.

Since a proper model is an exactly proportioned replica of what will be seen on the stage, it is the form of presentation which is most likely to be readable by a relatively visually illiterate eye. The major ability required to read a set designer's work is that of visual multiplication by 25 and to do this the eye is constantly helped by a reference point it can immediately understand — the human figure.

There will still be some surprises when the finalised setting appears on the stage. For the audience (and its rehearsal representatives, the production team) no model can fully provide the sensation of viewing from within the context of the theatre's auditorium. And no model can fully prepare the actors for being within the set rather than looking at it. Nevertheless, as their experience grows of relating model boxes to stages, all directors, actors and production personnel develop increasing accuracy in their own specialised version of the 25 factor. But designers should always have some accurate 1 : 25 human figures on hand, both for their own working process and for communicating with their team colleagues.

While the model is concerned essentially with the stage, it also needs to include some indication of that stage's orientation in relation to the audience. For a proscenium theatre this is a relatively simple matter of framing the set with a proscenium arch. Such a frame is often made in simple black card, but if the performances are to be in a theatre with a distinctive proscenium, possibly ornately plastered and gilded, a truer impression may be gained by including this in the modelling. This is particularly so if part of the acting area thrusts through the proscenium arch. For any kind of open unframed arena staging, the model needs to find some way of showing how the acting space relates to the audience — certainly including the seating adjacent to the acting area and some indication of how it tiers from there.

It is possible to complete much of the design work in two-dimensional drawings and paintings (often known as renderings, especially in America) with the details of spatial relations set out in ground plan form. This design work can be

Rae Smith's design for Theatre de Complicité's *Street of Crocodiles* was created in rehearsal during four weeks of watching and drawing.

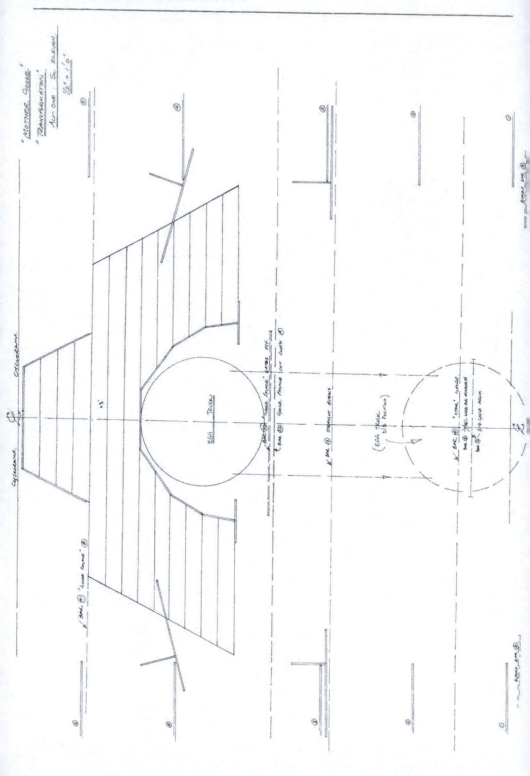

so complete that the model making becomes almost a formality with all the decisions made and recorded in drawings, or clearly pictured in the designer's mind.

But few designers like to work in this way. Most prefer to have a two-way relationship with a model which responds by leading the designer to consider alternatives. As individual components of the model are built, they influence the detailing of each other, with the designer simultaneously refining and checking that both the structure of the space and its visual aesthetic will work in support of the play. The reading, listening, researching, discussing, experimenting and discarding become a preparatory, but essential, phase to the real creative phase of working into the model — where the previously gathered and sifted ideas and information are transformed into a piece of visual art.

Light and easily worked materials such as card, balsa and wire are the essential stuff of model making, with scalpel and soldering iron prominent among the tools. Rigidity, stability and accuracy are essential qualities. The aim is to have as few imponderables as possible. It is very difficult to give a convincing demonstration of a model if one has to keep apologising that such and such a piece will be straighter, darker in tone or more strongly textured — and in a demonstration it can be highly irritating if bits keep falling over.

The importance of rigidity, stability and accuracy in demonstrating a model will be obvious whether the designer is trying to sell an idea to the director, or informing the team of enabling collaborators who will be responsible for multiplying it by 25 into reality. But it is also easier and more satisfying for the designer to work in a model that is stable and rigid; and without accuracy the eye cannot truly know whether or not details of form, colour and texture are just right.

Ground plans

A ground plan shows the position of everything on the stage. The base of all pieces standing on the stage floor is fully marked and the placing of items hung above the stage is indicated. Levels and steps can be given written indication of their height above stage level (e.g. + 1.35m; 4ft 4in) but a ground plan deals primarily with stage width and depth. This information is sufficient for most requirements of the director and choreographer. However, a cross-section through the centreline is helpful for them and essential for the lighting designer and stage management.

The drawing of a ground plan follows naturally from the model since the model includes all the information. However, there are times when it may be useful to make some of the geographical decisions in a ground plan either before or during the model making. And when time is tight, it can be useful for the director, and

Ground plan for a scene from the Christmas pantomime *Mother Goose* at the King's Theatre, Edinburgh (designed by Terry Parsons) showing permanent masking portals, positions of flown and set pieces for this scene, and starting/finishing positions for a motorised truck.

possibly the lighting designer, to have ground plans to allow them to commence work before the final model is completed.

Bauprobe

At a point when the details of the proposed configuration of the stage space are becoming clear, it can be very useful to experiment with a full scale mock-up on the stage. This allows director, choreographer and design team to test the space by walking it. Such a bauprobe (or 'build rehearsal') is standard in central European repertoire theatres, where it allows minor adjustments in dimensions to be tried to encourage possible use of elevators and stock rostra. Such changes may be acceptable to the designer and save a considerable amount of money in both initial production and daily running costs.

Continuing debate

Throughout the modelling process, just as throughout the entire preparation and rehearsal period, ideas will come and go with everyone needing to retain flexibility. The developing model may trigger a fresh idea for the director which may in turn stimulate the designer to respond by modifying or amplifying a visual aspect. The debate is continuous.

Storyboard

Demonstrating the detailed progress of the proposed use of a stage setting through time and place is not easy. Changes involving scenery repositioning are relatively straightforward to show. But changes are more difficult when they depend upon lighting or upon the way in which acting scenes are placed within the context of the total stage environment. Such demonstrations are not only an integral part of the general debate within the production team, they are also a necessary aid for designers to sell their ideas so that their designs are used in the way that they are convinced will be right for the play.

A method gaining increasing popularity is to support the model with a storyboard sequence of drawings. These can, and perhaps generally ought, to be rather impressionistic in style. They include the appropriate elements of the set and furnishings in position, and actors in the proposed areas of the stage to be used. Storyboard drawings are usually rather too small to carry any significant costume detail but it is useful if there is an indication of which of their costumes the actors are wearing.

Ideally there should be some indication of light — particularly showing the areas of stage where the light is concentrated, the direction of its source, and its tonal quality. Light is perhaps the least easy element to include in such a drawing. But, on the principle that it is light that provides visibility, some designers have found it useful to use black paper as the starting point for drawing. However, one of the simplest ways of producing the large numbers of drawings required in complex storyboards is to superimpose changes on a photocopied outline image of the basic fixed elements of the set.

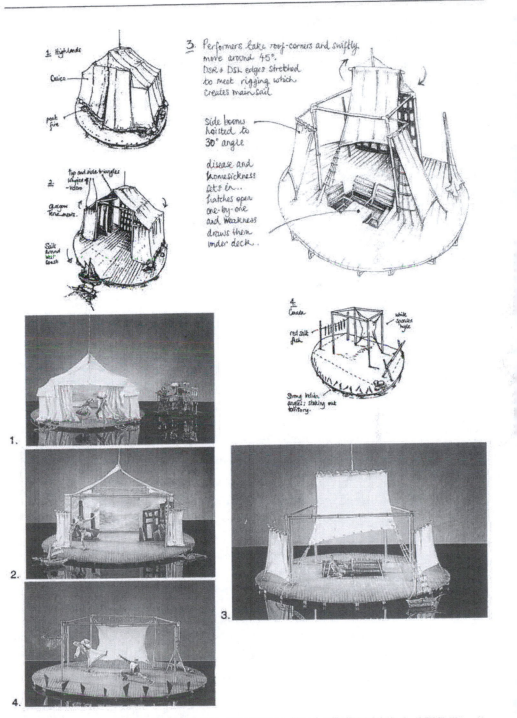

Kate Borthwick's priority in designing *Desperate Journey*, for touring by TAG Theatre Company, was to create four distinct worlds: a visual difference between the soft, weathered homeland of Scotland and the brave new world of Canada.

LIGHTING DESIGNER

The point where the lighting designer will become involved varies with the complexity of the production and the organisation producing it. The more a production style seeks to use light to indicate or to support changes in time and/or place, the earlier its lighting designer needs to be involved in the debate with set designer and director. In any such debate the lighting designer has two concerns:

* establishing the role of light in terms of visual style; and
* seeking the availability of optimum positions for placing lights to attain these stylistic objectives.

In a producing theatre with its own resident design team, it is easier for the discussion process to be ongoing and informal than when a freelance team has been assembled with a lighting designer who, at least during the earlier planning phases, is likely to be also working on another production elsewhere.

But the lighting designer should certainly be involved in a discussion with set designer and director (and choreographer if applicable) as soon as their ideas seem to be firming up, even if the proposed use of the stage space is still very tentative.

The extent of subsequent discussions during the development of the model will depend upon many interacting factors, particularly:

* The extent to which the team (particularly set and lighting designers) have already worked together on previous productions and the consequent under-standing that has developed between them.

* The complexity of the lighting style, particularly the extent of its departure from naturalism and its proposed use of light to define areas and shift emphasis.

* The physical complexity of the set, particularly rationalisation of flying space between possible conflicting scenic and lighting needs.

A major problem in all discussions involving lighting designers is that their design paperwork is in a diagrammatic form which bears no visual relationship to the light that will appear on stage. Since it is difficult to see any solution to this (other than perhaps lighting designers acquiring improved drawing and painting skills), there is a justified worry throughout all lighting discussions that members of the production team may be interpreting different visual meanings from a particular wording.

PRODUCTION TEAM AGREEMENT

When the model is near to finalisation in its functional form, although possibly (and perhaps preferably) still being worked into for the detailed visual treatment, there is need for an extended meeting to include all designers, director, (choreographer) and production manager. This will involve going through the complete function of the model in detail and in sequence, discussing the likely placing of scenes and contribution of lighting. Looking in this way at specific moments in the play's action will trigger much cross-questioning which should, in turn, help to identify potential problems and stimulate decisions about alternative solutions.

The lighting designer's experienced eye will be able to offer help with the prediction of how tightly certain scenes can be lit, particularly the problem of face versus floor, and the consequences of reflections from surface treatments. The lighting designer may suggest some darkening or increased texturing of areas which are likely to collect so much light that they will need compensation in order to appear at the toning level desired by the set designer.

The lighting designer will already have considered the colour and texture of the costumes, both in relation to the set and to any use of coloured light inherent in the production's proposed visual style. Now is the time to check, while going through in sequence, which costumes will be worn in each scene and the colour toning of the light, considering both the response of the costumes individually, and their relation to each other and to the set.

If all basic problems are not resolved at this meeting, it will need to be subsequently reconvened, after breaks for all parties to go away and rethink, on as many occasions as are necessary. It is essential that a completed design offers at least a fail-safe solution, possibly with several riskier options, for staging the play in a manner that will handle its mechanics in a visually supportive way.

MODEL APPROVAL

The agreement of the director and the entire design team is a necessary basis towards model approval. However, there are other people who need to be involved before the designs can be accepted to go forward for realisation.

If a new play, the writer should certainly be shown out of courtesy, even if this is not a contractual right. And similarly the leading actors. Anyway, writers and actors can often put their finger on something that the production team have missed. The producer, or whatever the title of the person carrying out the producer's function of assembling the package of script, cast, production team, theatre and budgets, will certainly wish to be seen exercising a right to approve, and is quite likely to have established a contractual right to do so. And a producer having, almost by definition, deep faith in the work can also offer positive comment. This producer approval will be important to the director/designer team who not only need the comfort of such approval but may well wish the design to be so highly regarded that extra funds will be made available to avoid the budgetary cutbacks being called for by that key model approver, the production manager.

In many ways, approval marks the completion of the design process. The major decisions have been made and are about to be realised in a 'multiplied 25 times' form that can only be undone with relatively enormous expenditure of time and money. But the success of the realisation, and therefore of the design, will depend

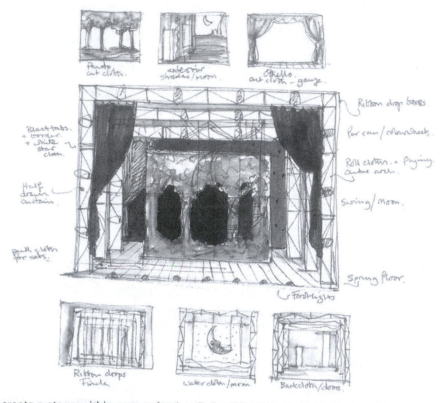

To create a stage within a stage for *Les Enfants du Paradis*, Paul Dart used trussing lagged with fabric to make it look old. All the flying, swings and drop cloths were operated from within the trussing framework, enabling a complex show to be toured easily.

upon the aesthetic input of all the artists who pursue their specialist crafts under the leadership of the design team. And that design team must, of course, retain flexibility throughout the entire process of design realisation, possibly reshaping and certainly fine tuning their visual response to the words and music as the production develops in the rehearsal room.

7 DESIGN REALISATION

Except in the smallest fringe productions whose rock bottom budgeting imposes a basically do-it-yourself approach, the designer's role in making sets, costumes and props is essentially one of supervision. It is a time when a designer is constantly pressed for instant decisions. There are days when the queue of specialist makers requiring immediate answers to alternative materials or methods seems longer than a multiple choice examination paper. How well the designer answers these questions will be one major factor in the successful realisation of the design. The other is watching progress and intervening positively when some aspect of the design is being misinterpreted.

Designers ability to do both of these effectively is primarily dependent upon their artist's eye. An important back-up to this sensibility is the personal experience bank built up by doing various support jobs in early career years and by continuous observation of specialists at work.

But fundamental to the exercise of all such abilities is the designer's personal relationships with the team of craft specialists who enable the designs to be realised. These specialists are sensitive artists who deserve to be treated as creative colleagues. Inevitably, their acuteness of perception will vary and this requires a high degree of personal awareness and caring response on the part of the designer.

SCENERY

The first major step towards set building is working drawings. Just how much of this is the responsibility of the designer will depend upon national practice and, within that, the practice of individual producing organisations.

In America a number of factors, including unionisation and a highly structured theatre design education within the universities, has tended to stress the craft aspects of designing rather more than in Europe. Consequently there is an expectancy in the USA that designers will be experienced in 'drafting' — the technique of preparing detailed working drawings for the construction shops.

In Britain there are wide variations of expectancy between the designer producing fully detailed working drawings and leaving all that in the hands of a drawing office within the production organisation or scenery contractors. More common, however, is the middle ground where the designer's working drawings break the set down into dimensioned pieces with the fine details of construction left to the shop. This is particularly so when sets are built from the wide range of

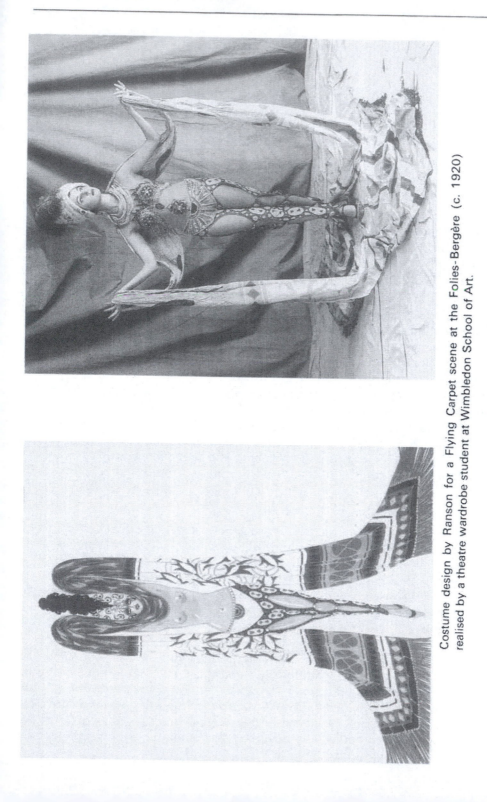

Costume design by Ranson for a Flying Carpet scene at the Folies-Bergère (c. 1920) realised by a theatre wardrobe student at Wimbledon School of Art.

materials which have replaced the canvas covered flat frames that were so long standard. (When flats are used today, the frames are covered with skin ply, although canvas may then be glued over the ply for texture.)

Whether or not the designer is responsible for working drawings, there does need to be a clear understanding between shop and designer as to the set's materials and its general structural quality in terms of solidity and delicacy. Particularly as this is an area where small financial savings can result in quite drastic reductions of visual quality.

A designer's closest contact with scenic preparations tends to be during the painting; in smaller theatres, the designer is quite likely to get personally involved with the brushes.

(In the 1960s and 1970s the prevailing visual styles were heavily dependent upon the use of natural materials with treatment limited to staining or texturing. During this time the demand for pictorial painting was so diminished that there is virtually a missing generation of scenic artists with the necessary experience. However, the use of paint has now revived sufficiently to ensure rediscovery and preservation of the old skills.)

The aim must be to prepare as much as possible before the set goes to the stage. Few workshops or scenic studios have enough space for erecting a full set, but hopefully it will be possible to assemble sections to check physical compatibility and visual matching between adjoining pieces.

PROPS

While the need for many of the props can be identified during the design period, many requirements will only evolve during rehearsal. To accommodate this, a designer needs to maintain contact with the rehearsal room, liaising through the stage management. In British theatre the key member of stage management is the *Deputy Stage Manager* who records all the actors' moves in the prompt book and is the reference point for all details of the evolving production. One of the assistant stage managers is usually assigned to look after props during rehearsal, and therefore becomes a valuable reference point for the director's and actors' expectations regarding size and practicalities. The use of approximates as substitute 'rehearsal props' is a useful method of establishing precise need.

For a contemporary play most props are likely to be bought rather than made, although 'breaking down' techniques may be required to make such props look used rather than new. A designer has to be ready to produce instant design drawings, either to help shoppers or for propmakers to work from. It is a characteristic of rehearsals that all new ideas are deemed by directors and actors to require immediate implementation.

COSTUME

The key person in the organisation of costume preparation is the *Costume Supervisor* who should be early identified amongst the staff of a permanent organisation or employed when the production is being assembled as a special package. For a modern play some of the clothes may be selected from standard retail shop stock. When clothes are being made it is likely that several costume workshops will be involved, particularly for specialised areas such as period tailoring and millinery. With fabric to be bought and possibly dyed and/or painted, accessories to be assembled and fittings to be arranged, wardrobe supervision demands considerable deployment of management skills.

While initial costume sketches may have been somewhat freely drawn to express total character rather than fine detail, the final designs are likely to show rather more precise indications of line, cut and trimmings. Just how diagrammatic should be the costume design handed over to the costumier is a matter of some debate in which personal preference plays a major part. Much depends upon the relationship between the designer and the cutter who has to interpret the drawing. Although final designs are frequently 'swatched' by pinning samples of material to the drawing, the designer will normally wish to have considerable involvement in the buying of the material and, if appropriate, its dyeing.

There will be discussion in varying depths, about cut. But the critical time for the designer to monitor this will be during assembly on dress stands and fittings with the actors. (At the heart of any wardrobe department schedule is the need for on-time completion of casting to provide actor measurements.) Between fittings a designer will be supervising progress, and then finally the vital breaking down, with varying degrees of subtlety, according to the wear which a particular costume would have been subjected to.

All the clothes come together at the Dress Parade when the actors wear each of their costumes in sequence for inspection by designer and director. The dress parade is normally held towards the end of the rehearsal room period when the production is just about to move on to the stage, although sometimes it is delayed until immediately prior to the first technical dress rehearsal. Whenever held, ideally it should take place in a theatre under stage lighting so that the costumes can also be assessed from a distance, particularly when checking how costumes for a scene relate to each other.

At the end of the dress parade it is inevitable that the costume supervisor will have reams of notes from director, choreographer, designer and the actors themselves, on many matters pertaining both to visual appearance and practicalities — particularly regarding comfort and quick changes. The alteration lists may seem enormous: keeping the situation stable and happy usually requires a priority list which puts the completion of actor and director practicalities before designer visuals.

LIGHTING

Realisation of the lighting design cannot begin until the production has possession of the stage with the completed scenery in position. However, this does give the lighting design some flexibility, and can adapt in response to the production's evolution in rehearsal.

Because the time slot for lighting is so tight and so close to the dress rehearsals and first performance, it is imperative that everything possible be done to prepare equipment, since poorly maintained lights can wreck any schedule. Equipment preparation is the organisational responsibility of the *Production Electrician* who, like the wardrobe supervisor, will be either a freelance or senior member of the producing theatre's resident staff. Most productions use a proportion of rented equipment (London's West End and New York's Broadway use only rented equipment) and very precise planning is required for the exact rigging requirements to be delivered for the fit-up.

That the lighting design cannot be seen to be developing during rehearsal can be a source of niggling worry both to the lighting designer and the rest of the production team. While all other aspects of the production can be seen increasingly to be taking shape, the lighting design remains a sheaf of plans whose graphics bear no visual resemblance to what will be seen on stage. Even when a very experienced lighting designer works with a team of long term associates, there will be moments of 'will he/she/I pull it out of the bag'. The only motto available is: 'Don't Panic'.

During the final week in the rehearsal room, when production shape is becoming firm and the schedule increasingly includes run-throughs interspersed among detailed work on specific scenes, the lighting designer needs to prepare a list of proposed lighting cues. Ideally this will result from a discussion between director, (choreographer), design team and the member of the stage management team who will call the cues in performance. However, work pressures at this time sometimes preclude such a meeting and if this is so the lighting designer should circulate a proposed list for comment. (In general, theatre people tend to be inhibited by the challenge of a blank sheet of paper but will respond to an opportunity to edit a proposal.)

A lighting discussion at this point can be useful in clarifying details of the progression from one scene to the next. Earlier discussion during the pre-rehearsal design phase will have agreed the beginning and end states of such changes, but may have left the precise sequence of mechanics and timing to be worked out after the production has taken more positive shape in rehearsal.

GET-IN and FIT-UP

All preparations, in rehearsals and workshops, are scheduled to peak on the eve of the day when the production takes possession of the stage. At this point every designer knows moments of insecurity based on, at best, whether the design was any good in the first place, and whether it has been able to adapt to rehearsal developments. If the rehearsals have been less than smooth, a designer may harbour thoughts, verging on paranoia, that other members of the team, particularly the director, neither appreciate nor understand the potential of the designs and are failing to make full use of the opportunities offered. However, the schedule between get-in and performance is usually so tight that there is minimal contingency for the unforeseen, let alone for experiment. And certainly not for paranoia. Once the ball rolls, the degree of concentration required by everyone is totally absorbing. Providing all preparations are complete (and this alas is less frequent than it ought to be) there is little for designers to do on stage during the early phases of fitting-up sets and lights except watch and fret. Unless, of course, this is a fringe or small informal theatre production when the designers will be in there doing it. But in a professional show of any size it is better to let the technicians get on with it, working from the plans. However, the designer should be present, since even the most careful documentation raises questions and is capable of misinterpretation.

There will be many demands on the designer at this time, particularly if one designer is responsible for both set and costumes. So, in reality, supervision of the fit-up usually means remaining within call and periodically keeping an eye on the progress. Once the set has been erected, the designer and stage manager can position the furniture, compromising if necessary between visual and actor movement needs. Whether all the scene changes are set and marked before lighting or whether the two processes are integrated will depend on the technical complexity of the production.

FOCUSING

In tandem with building the set, work will have been in progress to hang the lights. Each one now has to be pointed at its predetermined area and carefully focused for size and quality.

Big repertoire theatres have their lights mounted on access bridges to speed focusing during the daily changeovers. And there is a growing use of remotely operated spotlights with motor control of essential movements. (The huge capital investment may be justified by savings in running costs.) However, focusing for most of us, certainly of the lights hanging over the stage, involves repositioning ladders to reach each spotlight. Normal practice uses a wheeled ladder called a tallescope which can be moved while the electrician remains aloft. When focusing, a lighting designer is concerned with how the light hits the actor, and its effect on the scenery. The quickest method is for the lighting designer to stand in each relevant actor position with back to the light — the effect of light on the set can then be easily seen, while a full body shadow confirms a lit actor.

Focusing is more precise if the stage is in darkness except for the light currently being worked on. And it helps if the lighting crew do not have to shout above the din of power tools and piano tuners. However, late running schedules can mean carpenters working in pools of light (hopefully away from the areas currently being focused), although most set designers develop a flair for working around the light designer, dressing their sets with the aid of ever shifting reflected light.

With focusing complete, the lighting can be composed. The standard method is for the lighting designer, sitting in mid-stalls with the rest of the design team, choreographer and director, to plot the lighting using an intercom to talk to the control room. The deputy stage manager stands by with the prompt book, checking the cue placing, while ASMs take up actor positions to assist balancing. This is a time of discovery: during all the discussions, did everyone interpret words as having the same visual meaning? It is also inevitably a time when compromises, hopefully only a few, are likely to be necessary between the director's priority for actors' faces and the set designer's concern for the total visual picture. Furthermore, a choreographer will be most concerned with good sculptural body lighting and a costume designer with clearly visible details of the clothes.

The lighting designer has to achieve a compromise and display tact in getting it accepted, knowing that balances agreed during lighting rehearsals without actors are likely to require some rebalancing during the first rehearsal with them. However, traditional lighting rehearsals have increasingly been modified by the advent of computerised controls with a capability for instant memorising of lighting states. Much of the fine balancing can now be carried out during actor orientation rehearsals on the set, with formal lighting rehearsals, if held at all, reduced to roughing in major pictures.

TECHNICAL REHEARSALS

With scenic fit-up completed and lighting plotted, the *techs* are the most important rehearsals for the design team. They are often called *stagger-throughs*, having continuous stops and no going forward until each problem has been solved. Actors and directors in a tech are concerned not with interpretation but with mechanics. The practicalities of wearing and changing costumes, making entrances and exits, moving around furniture, and getting the feel of the theatre and level of projection required for both character and voice. Detailed timing of scene and light changes has to be integrated with acting and sound. The process can be very long and inevitably induces raw nerves, particularly as there is a general feeling of time running out. Which, of course, it is!

This is a very dangerous time for designers. Panic can lead to difficult but potentially effective uses of the set being sacrificed before their trickier aspects have been solved with adequate rehearsals. Designers need to keep that quiet but determined cool which will help them to insist on complex sequences being given a full chance with properly detailed rehearsal before they are abandoned. However, there may be a need to apply creative flexibility in finding a modification that will enable the idea to work in a simplified yet almost as effective form.

At the end of the technical rehearsal, everyone — production team, actors and technicians — should be clear about what is supposed to happen. And its timing. Anyone responsible for making something happen should be reasonably confident that it can be made to happen with the agreed timing, subject to further rehearsal.

Everyone will have a sheaf of notes of things to be put right, and in selecting priorities it is once again necessary to give priority to mechanical matters affecting the running of the show rather than to correcting visual things which are causing great anguish to the artist's eye of the designer. The skills of a good production manager are vital for the integration of all the work to be done at this time.

DRESS REHEARSALS

Dress rehearsals will hopefully just be a time for polishing the timing, fine balancing the lights, and observing the growing improvements in visual quality as a result of daily touching up. And, of course, making notes for even more work. There may be a crisis. Alas this may be because so many theatre people seem to savour a crisis. It is vital to avoid panic. But if there is a serious problem then it should be tackled right away. The real difficulty is recognising a genuine problem rather than dealing with it. Diagnosis and cure depend to some extent upon experience, but perhaps rather more upon the designer's innate artistry and eye.

PERFORMANCE

First nights are rarely enjoyable. The production team can feel that the child is no longer theirs. There is anguish as every tricky moment approaches, relief as it is successfully passed. The reward is a clutch of those moments of magic which allow any artist the pleasure of temporarily suspending that innate self-criticism which daily sustains their motivation.

8 DESIGNING WITH NEW TECHNOLOGIES

Computer processing of information is probably the most revolutionary factor currently influencing the way we live. The storage, retrieval and processing of words and numbers has become common place and the programming of computers to generate and manipulate visual images is becoming increasingly sophisticated.

The use of CAD and CAM — *computer aided design* and *computer aided manufacture* — is growing in many sectors of industry. Television adverts for the motor industry have made us familiar with the concept of producing design drawings on a video screen and then assembling the car with the aid of computer programmed robotic tools.

What are the prospects for theatre design?

COMPUTER AIDED REALISATION

Information technology is more commonly used in the realisation of theatre designs than in the design process itself. Since the mid-1970s, data processing has been the standard method of storing lighting states and retrieving them for playback during performance. This instant memorising and recall has speeded up the lighting process, increased its accuracy and opened up new horizons of fluidity.

These computer lighting controls do not make lighting decisions. They have not replaced any of the lighting designer's work at the drawing board. But they do offer a new freedom in realisation — a freedom to use time more creatively. More experimentally. And, perhaps most importantly, to try an idea and reject it. Quickly.

Computers are being applied to other areas of stage technology, particularly to some aspects of sound mixing and to scenic movements. The indications from experiments in computer control of flying systems are that we can look to new degrees of sophistication in finely proportioned timing. Like the lighting controls, these devices will not do anything that could not be done with extremely long detailed rehearsing by a large number of trained technicians. But we are rarely able either to schedule the time or to budget for the technicians.

Apart from such developments, the theatre's use of computers is mostly for standard information handling. Box office ticket sales are integrated with accountancy systems which increasingly are incorporated within complete management systems. Although such systems have so far been concerned mostly

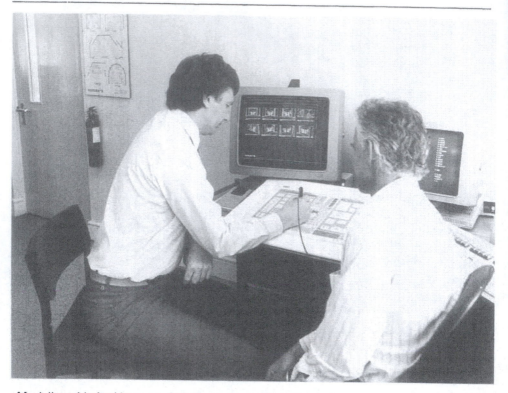

Modelbox Limited is a specialist computer aided design facility based in the centre of London's West End theatreland. Auditorium sightline information and stage plans for most British theatres are stored in software for instant retrieval in a system which includes computer drafting and plan print-out.

with financial control and marketing, there is a growth in the availability and use of software programs for production management. These include stock control in scenic and wardrobe workshops, inventory control of prop and wardrobe stores, and programs which calculate, list and cost, for example, total timber or filter requirements in each size category.

COMPUTER AIDED DESIGN

The key word is *aided*: computers cannot design but they can offer various possibilities of assistance to the designer. Computers make logical decisions by processing information with which they have been fed. They are not capable of the imaginative illogical decisions that are fundamental to art. But they can service the designer's imagination through their capability for allowing information (verbal, numerical and visual) to be instantly recalled, manipulated and discarded. Let us examine the potential of this new technology in relation to some of the steps of the design process.

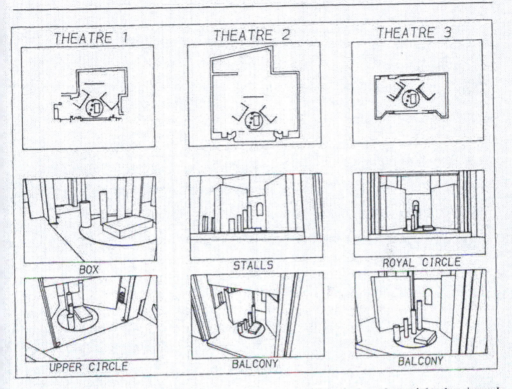

The *Modelbox Limited* computer is programmed to enable a designer's model to be viewed from various audience angles on the system's video screen, aiding assessment of potential sightline and masking problems.

Research

The amount of verbal and visual material stored in computerised data bases is growing continuously. However, user-demand has ensured a bias towards storing words rather than images. And there is possibly better cataloguing of word books than picture books. But this will change: comprehensive cataloguing first, followed by data banks of the actual pictures.

Computers are given commands through a letter and number keyboard and/or moving a pointer, called a cursor, around the screen. This cursor may be told where to go by keying or, perhaps more rationally for an artist, by moving a pencil-like device over a flat table surface in front of the screen. When comprehensive picture libraries become available, designers will have access to picture collections all over the world by keying in a code, or searching through a sequence of alternative pictograms with a cursor. By connecting a computer to their domestic telephone wires, designers will be able to work in any library anywhere. The facility may not yet be developed, but the technology exists. It is easier and cheaper to put an image in a data bank than record it on microfiche. And we need only recall how quickly the microfiche has become adopted for standard library cataloguing, and for storing bulky material like journals, to realise that digital access could develop rapidly for research in all fields including design.

Image manipulation

When an interesting image has been located, it can be manipulated on the screen. Depending upon the degree of sophistication of the computer system, it can be subjected to such treatment as:

* Zooming the size up and down in many ways from totally shrinking the entire image to blowing up a tiny selected section.

* Rotating the image in all planes to view from alternative angles.

* Adding line, texture or colour.

* Juxtaposing and superimposing a series of images.

The pictures need not, of course, come from an image library. Designers can 'draw' their own images on the screen and use computer manipulation as an additional technique. An external picture or object can be fed into the system by means of a video camera and a collection of such material can either be stored short term while work is in progress, or accumulated towards the formation of a designer's own personal working picture library.

Images from all these various sources may be combined, overlaid, proportioned, balanced and *rejected*.

Perhaps the rejection facility is the most important. The speed at which a visual idea may be developed and abandoned allows much experiment that could easily be inhibited by the time scale of more traditional design methods.

Image preparation

The images which appear on a video screen have, by the nature of the means of their production, a luminous quality. They tend to seem more suitable for projection than for realisation in physical materials. Indeed, computer graphics are particularly effective on television — so effective and so fast to prepare that they have almost totally replaced manual methods. However, when printed out and possibly worked into by other techniques, video generated images can become the decorative treatments for the surfaces of structural elements within the model.

Computers are just one of a series of newer techniques for image production. Photocopiers are very useful, particularly with reduction and enlarging facilities by such irregular factors as 1.5, in addition to the more usual straightforward doubling or halving by a factor of 2. Once again the images produced are likely to form a basis for being worked into with other techniques. The photographic processes of graphic design are also being increasingly employed, not just for copying and scaling but for printing textures and pictorial images on to all kinds of materials from fabrics to foils.

The model

All these processes offer two-dimensional support towards the spatial design work carried out in the model. Can any of this model box activity be transferred to the computer video screen?

With a video camera it is possible to put a work-in-progress model into a computer and then work on its screen image, rearranging the position of various pieces and experimenting with their relative scale. For a production where a projection surface is an integral part of the set, this technique is the only truly viable method of seeing the effect of projection in the model and selecting, scaling and cropping the artwork from which slides are to be made. (Using a video camera, each potential piece of artwork is stored in the computer memory. With the set on screen, each piece of artwork in turn is zoomed to match the area of the model's projection surface and can then be scaled, etc.

Although its screen is flat, a computer can not only generate and manipulate three-dimensional drawings but can draw them from alternative viewpoints. Thus it is possible to check sightlines from various parts of the theatre in order to find out just what the audience will see (or not see) from there.

Even the deepest crystal ball will find some credibility problems in predicting a theatre designer doing all the work in a computer then commanding that computer to make a model while the designer has dinner. Yet new processes now include building three-dimensional objects directly from a computer design by using a liquid plastic which solidifies under ultraviolet light. The object is built up from a series of thin layers, each drawn by a computer controlled light source which solidifies the liquid. It is difficult to believe that this technique could become sufficiently sophisticated for a complete stage model. But perhaps for shaping the structure of pieces to be further worked on in the model box?

Plans
Plans and elevations of the design can be printed directly from the information in the computer. And it is possible to break a set down into component parts and produce working drawings for each.

Storyboards
The use of a screen to demonstrate the way a set is intended to be used in performance can include showing a sequence of moments from the progress of the set through time — or even an animated sequence of the changes in action.

Costume design
Computer programs for the garment manufacturing industry have been adapted for use in theatre costume workshops. For example, a computer can plan how to lay out pattern pieces to make the most economic use of fabric width and then calculate the lengths required.

Costume design is the area of theatre design where an artist's traditional drawing and painting techniques are used in their purest and freest form, and seem totally appropriate. However, computer techniques have been developed whereby an authentic period costume drawing is brought to the screen and transformed into a production costume design through the designer working into the image with an electronic pencil or brush.

Lighting design

There are software programs to assist a lighting designer to relate:

- position of spotlight;

- angle at which light will hit the actor;

- area of stage lit and extent of shadow thrown on any scenery in that area.

This is shown in graphic form on the video screen. Earlier programs, in two dimensions, used drawings similar to the roughs that a designer working traditionally might make on a scrap pad, to assist decisions of where to place lights on the main lighting layout plan. More recent programs can, however, display in the form of a three-dimensional drawing. Potential advantage to the designer is the instant response of the computer drawing. As the cursor is used to shift the spotlight position, the angle of the light striking an actor, and the length of the shadow, immediately change in consequence. And if the spotlight's beam angle is keyed in, the area lit will also automatically change in size as the distance between spotlight and stage is altered.

Software programs are in an advanced state of development for the computer visualisation of stage lighting on a video screen which displays pictorial images of costumed figures in the stage setting. These programs allow the direction, colour and intensity of the light to be manipulated on the screen to the same extent that it can be controlled in the theatre.

Quality of visualisation is approaching *what you see on the screen, you can get on the stage*, so that the viewer's eye need compensate only for the differing luminosity of the video and stage images.

DESIGN TOOL OR GIMMICK?

How useful are the new technologies? To most of us older designers, they seem to lack the tactile quality of our traditional pens, brushes and blades. To us, computerspeak is an alien language whose unfamiliarity breeds mistrust and suspicion. But today's school leavers are increasingly sophisticated in the ways of the new technologies. To many of them, keyboards and cursors are familiar tools. They 'boot' computers in the same routine way that we elders sharpen pencils. The end rather than the means is important: time will tell.

9 LEARNING TO DESIGN

How does one become a theatre designer? Like all jobs in the theatre there is no single route: designers learn by various mixes of formal and informal methods. It is possible to design professionally for theatre without any formal training in theatre design, or indeed in theatre or art, by just relying on talent and observation. But even the most splendid natural talent can usually benefit from a situation structured to encourage personal development through discovery.

I would suggest that the following personal qualities seem desirable in a theatre designer:

* Strong visual imagination.
* Ability to express and communicate this through various media, especially drawing.
* Wide interest in people, their relationships with each other and with their environment, both in reality and as reflected in all the arts, today and throughout history.
* Commitment to theatre.
* Personal ability to relate to, and work with, the other members of the creative and interpretative team that constitutes a theatre.

Is a theatre designer a visual artist who works in theatre, or a theatre person who specialises in the visual aspects of production? During my own working lifetime, I have gradually shifted my viewpoint from the latter to the former and am now convinced (or as convinced as any open minded arts worker should permit themselves to be about anything) that the priorities for theatre design education are the development of:

(1) A visual awareness feeding a visual imagination, coupled to an ability to communicate through drawing and other media.

(2) An ability to probe the words and music of a dramatic text in search of a response which is both a visual metaphor for the text and a support for the actors in their interpretation of it through performance.

(3) An understanding of the technical means of costuming actors, and of constructing a scenic environment and manipulating its space through a progression of time.

THEATRE DESIGN STUDY OPTIONS

The above priorities tend to be difficult to incorporate in traditional educational systems which tend to be biased towards technical means rather than artistic end. The structure of formal education is generally focused towards qualification, and this implies examinations. However, some aspects of a subject are easier to examine than others, so the curriculum may emphasise these aspects, particularly if they are easier to teach.

Universities

Most higher education, particularly that centred in universities, is based on verbal analysis. There is a determination to 'explain' music and painting by endeavouring to translate their own special non-verbal languages into words. Original imaginative thinking is rarely encouraged: emphasis tends to be placed on analysing the thoughts of others with a view to the comparisons and contrasts which lead to logical decisions.

Drama schools

In almost complete contrast to the university concentration upon verbal analysis stands the drama school practical approach, with a series of fully staged productions at the core of its educational philosophy. A major problem of this approach is that teaching of design stands in danger of becoming secondary to servicing the acting course. In view of the designer's supportive role in relation to the actor, this is virtually inevitable. But a student designer's need to experience the pressures of preparation for a performance deadline should be balanced within a programme structure where performance work and exploratory studies feed each other.

Art schools

In my view this can most successfully be accomplished within the framework of an Art School, provided that productions are undertaken in collaboration with a wide range of performing groups.

Art schools have been developed to cope with the special educational needs of visual thinkers. They acknowledge that the artist designer processes information in visual rather than verbal form and, rather than submit it to logical analysis, transforms it by a creative act. The nature of this creative act is not something that can be explained by the artist, although an entire industry of critics and art historians has long devoted itself to attempts at verbalising it on the artist's behalf.

Art schools, because they have a tradition of staffing by artists rather than analysts, are geared to fostering the kind of personal development that leans towards an ability to make creative decisions. This is a finely structured process involving placing students in situations where they can make discoveries. This structure acknowledges not only that different students will develop at a different pace, but that discovery can come with a surge, often following a long fallow period of search.

Art school examining systems place more emphasis on debate within the assessment team about the visual quality of work produced than on marks gained either by formal testing or accumulated from projects. Indeed, many art teachers are very reluctant to apply a continuous assessment marking system to project work, since it would inevitably inhibit the free debate amongst students about each other's work that is such a valuable feature of the critical evaluation sessions at the end of each project. And since such a 'crit' is similar to the way in which professional theatre designers present their work to the rest of the production team, it is surely to be seen as an interim rather than a final phase in the project. The time to assess theatre design students is when they place their work on end-of-year public exhibition — an equivalent of performance.

Art schools do not normally include courses in acting or in other theatre studies. This gives them the freedom to undertake productions in collaboration with a wide range of performance groups rather than be limited to designing for productions which tend to have been chosen to foster the talents of a drama school's acting students or to explore the alternative theories of dramatic structure and performance which are central to the theatre studies programme of a university.

Siting theatre design students in an art school has the advantages of daily contact with students from other areas of the fine and applied arts. On the other hand, theatre is a team art and to isolate its design students can only work against the fostering of the interaction which is central to performance.

There are several possible modes of locating theatre design studies within an art school. One is by the study of a non-theatre oriented art discipline — probably fine art (i.e. drawing and painting) — as a preliminary to a concentrated post-graduate course in theatre design. Another is a post-experience course geared for those who have already had professional experience in other branches of theatre. Most students however are likely to approach their study through taking one of the standard three year courses of the higher educational system, geared to a normal entry at 17 to 19. But to prepare themselves for this it is highly desirable that they avail themselves of one of the finest features of the art school system — *a foundation course.*

Foundation courses

Foundation courses provide a general introduction to art. They include a lot of drawing and painting and introduce students to handling a diverse range of media. These courses are partly diagnostic in character, helping students to confirm not only that they really want to proceed but in which area of art and design they wish to specialise. A particular strength is the way in which they give students a total submersion in art and design: there is a world of difference between this and the art periods of a school timetable. Anyone interviewing students for art and design degree courses is aware of the enormous differences in creative maturity between those of similar natural talent who have experienced a foundation course and those who have not.

The future

Recent years have seen a massive expansion in course provision for all areas of theatre studies. For potential theatre designers, the study options have become increasingly similar in aims but more diverse in approach. Art schools and drama schools are tending to become more academic while universities are showing increasing orientation towards the pragmatic skill requirements of a professional career. The options have become so wide that individual students need to consider a wide range of course programmes in order to choose the study path with which they feel most comfortable. Perhaps, in reaching a decision, the fundamental question will be whether they tend to view themselves as an artist designer working in theatre or a theatre person who designs. Related to this will be a consideration of how the focus of a particular programme offers opportunities for an alternative career. The cruel reality of theatre education is that the theatre industry can only absorb a small proportion of the annual crop of theatre graduates.

THEATRE DESIGN COURSE STRUCTURE

How then should a theatre design course be structured? I would suggest:

The core study will be a series of projects where the design process is taken to a point just short of realisation. Although not following every design through to performance places the work in a somewhat artificial situation, a parallel series of projects throughout the course will use the stage and many will reach an audience. The earlier ones will be workshop situations particularly aimed at developing an awareness of stage space. Indeed, the very first might well be based on experimenting with the use of real space as an actor and then developing that experience by working on the same scene in 1 : 25 model form.

But as the course progresses, much of the stage work will become gradually more formalised as the students work as design assistants and then are given their own full design opportunities in collaborative productions between the design school and acting schools or small professional fringe companies.

Experiencing stage space as an actor is very important for student designers — as is wearing costumes they have made, and handling props of their own design and construction. So stage exploration should start with acting — particularly movement — in a workshop theatre situation, using both text and improvisation; props, costumes, sets and lights being devised according to need as a series of group activities.

It is important that the experience thus gained is used to feed studio design work in drawing and model form. Indeed, throughout the course there is a need for a structure which ensures cross-stimulation between stage and studio work. Throughout their course (and ideally during their subsequent career) students have need of opportunities of returning to a stage to experiment, perhaps even occasionally forgetting the actors and devising an entertainment based purely on static or mobile objects transformed through a progression of time. They should also be encouraged to use an empty space (ideally a bare stage) to stake out proposed difficult acting areas from their model boxes in order to try placing acting scenes in them. Some coloured tape and the simplest of found objects such as chairs can be used, although it is useful to have some stock modular folding rostra available for establishing levels.

But no stage or studio activity can proceed in a constructive manner unless the student is also simultaneously acquiring a knowledge of the techniques of staging, of modelling and of research. There is a lot of basic information to be absorbed very quickly, and particular care needs to be taken to ensure that it is injected into the course in the right sequence and at the right pace.

First-year students of Theatre Design at the Central School of Art and Design in *About a Painter*, a stage exercise based on the life and work of Casper Neher whose theatre designs were a major influence on Brecht. The project, devised and directed by Pamela Howard, explored stage space and provided an opportunity to acquire basic skills in costume, set, prop and lighting technologies.

Stage studies

Whenever possible, it is desirable that students are placed in a situation where they can discover the need for information. Experimental stage exercises in the use of space and time can be devised so that they involve the need to find out about such practicalities as methods of construction and support of scenic pieces, propmaking, painting and flying. In a largish group it can be difficult for everyone to learn simultaneously through 'hands on' experience and it is almost inevitable that different people will make discoveries in different areas and initially acquire different skills. Accordingly, there is a need to share and expand discovery by a follow up with slide lectures showing the various techniques used in wider and different circumstances. For this video recordings would seem to offer a method, hitherto virtually unexploited, of demonstrating stage and workshop techniques in the classroom.

Costume studies

Some costume studies will evolve naturally from stage experiments. But the basic information needed to approach costume designing requires integrated theoretical and practical studies, with the history of cutting at their core. A systematic formal study of the cut of clothes across the centuries will focus on the clothes normally worn by people in various layers of society. It should include some study of clothes as seen through the eyes of painters as well as through the reality of museum collections. Such a course should be taught by a practising costume designer familiar with the way in which street clothes are transformed into stage costumes through various degrees of heightening while remaining faithful to period. Linked to this will be practical sessions in cutting period patterns and in costume assembly. Life drawing classes should include the human figure not only naked but in period clothes and corset.

Lighting studies

An awareness of light should be encouraged from the very beginning of stage project work. Lighting discoveries are made by observation of cause and effect and initially this is easier if the number of variables is kept to a minimum. A designer's prime interest is the consequences of the angle at which light strikes an object or actor. So, after basic instruction in safe handling (electrical and mechanical) of equipment, students should have access to a symmetrical grid of spotlights offering a reasonably comprehensive choice of angles. Initially all the spots should be identical and of the simplest (probably fresnel) type. More elaborate spotlight types should only be introduced when the need for their various sophisticated adjustments has been established through practical discovery.

Experiments should be structured to explore the lighting of objects and then of actors; followed by the crucial interaction between light for actor and light for environment (starting with such very basic exercises as lighting a pillar then lighting an actor, followed by the actor standing in front of the pillar). Once some mastery of directional white light has been achieved, exploration can be widened to include colour.

Design projects

Once a basic grounding has begun to be established, by such structured discovery studies in the use of costume, stage space and light, design projects can be undertaken in a manner similar to the professional process. To reflect the designer's normal working relationships, projects should be directed by people who are primarily theatre directors. Tutorial support comes from experienced designers, and various specialists help by a constructive playing of their normal role. The design projects throughout a course should embrace a mix of different scales of dramatic and musical works from a wide range of periods, including new unperformed writing.

Precise budget targets can act as an inhibiting distraction to an embryonic designer, but projects should be carried through on a budgetary scale appropriate to the normal operations of the theatre which has been specified. Students should always be expected to defend high cost options on artistic grounds and this will be part of the verbal articulacy with which they will be encouraged to present their work.

Designs for productions to be carried through into performance will, of course, be very much subject to a finely controlled budget with responsibility placed firmly with the student designer. But such productions are likely to be on a smaller scale than most of the studio projects and their budgeting will accordingly make reasonable demands on the student's experience.

A THEATRE DESIGN COURSE PHILOSOPHY

The suggested philosophy for any course in theatre design is that the students should be regarded as the younger colleagues of the professional designers who teach them — and in the art school tradition these teachers will be part-timers drawn from the ranks of practising professionals. As far as possible courses should operate according to the processes of standard professional theatre practice, with the addition of a supportive structure which places students in appropriate situations for decision making. They should be encouraged to live dangerously in taking artistic risks, but discouraged from any approach which seeks uniqueness at the expense of serving the actors' attempt to communicate the writer's work to the audience.

10 CRITICAL EVALUATION

An artist's self-evaluation is a continuous process since virtually every work decision depends upon a qualitative judgement rather than a logical response. Theatre designers, like all visual artists, must rely upon their eye to judge the internal quality of their work. But evaluation of a designer's contribution to a production poses a sequence of many interrelated questions.

Theatre colleagues are notoriously unreliable critics. While discussions during the design process will be open and constructive, they are likely to be overtaken by the stage's traditional gushing insincerity on opening night. Newspaper criticism may be gratifying, irritating or depressing but its analysis is unlikely to be sufficiently detailed to be of much help. There will usually be a couple of close friends who can be relied upon for honest and informed comment, but most designers are dependent upon self-criticism for any detailed analysis of the effectiveness of their contribution to the production.

Any such evaluation is based upon self-questioning and the questions to be asked after the first performance are related to the effectiveness of decisions taken by the design team during the various phases of the production process. Ideally the design team would sit down for a frank open post mortem discussion, which would subsequently be joined by the director and members of the enabling team. But this is very very rare outside a formal educational environment.

However, the process of self-education which is continuous throughout a theatre designer's career is dependent upon self-analysis and the following is offered as the skeleton of an agenda for self (or group!) evaluation to be adapted for individual use.

AGENDA FOR A POST MORTEM

How well did the designs serve the production?
- In aims?
- In the achievement of these aims?
- In their realisation?

How good were the style decisions?
- How successfully did the chosen style reveal depths without introducing distortions?
- Did the designs support the actors in interpreting the script and/or score?
- Did they offer an appropriate visual metaphor for the words and/or music?

* Were some aspects of the piece stressed at the expense of others?
* Did the approach create more problems than it solved?
* Did the style hit an appropriate departure from naturalism?
* Was the approach consistent throughout?
* Did set, costumes, props and lighting styles all integrate?
* Was the production style compatible with the architecture of the theatre?

Did we get our priorities right?
* Or was there too much concentration on some moments to the detriment of others?

How was the set?
* Did it offer environmental support to the actors? Or were they too exposed?
* Was it sufficiently flexible in support of the time dimension?
* How good was the placing of the individual scenes?
* Did it support the costumes?
* How well did it respond to light?

How were the props?
* Were they what the characters would have used?
* Did they look natural? Or contrived?

How were the costumes?
* Did they convince as clothes that the characters would have worn?
* Were they sufficiently in period? Or anachronistic to a degree incompatible with the production style?
* Did they hit the right heightening of reality?
* Did they show appropriate wear?

How was the lighting?
* Did the palette of focused lights provide everything the director and the rest of the design team hoped for?
* Was it too naturalistic? Or not naturalistic enough?
* Could it have been more atmospheric?
* Or more selective?

How closely did the performance match the original discussions?
* Were there differences due to changes in ideas as the production developed in rehearsal?
* If so, were we flexible enough in observing these changes and adapting the design?

How was the realisation?
* Could sets, props and costumes have been better made?
* Were there technical problems with the lighting equipment?
* Did stage fit-up and light focusing progress smoothly?
* Were the costumes all completed (apart from minor adjustments) in time?
* Were problems caused by the architecture of the theatre?

SOME SUGGESTIONS FOR FURTHER READING

THEATRE DESIGN

Make Space! — design for theatre and alternative spaces (Design Umbrella in association with The Society of British Theatre Designers, London)

Arnold Aronson: *The History and Theory of Environmental Scenography* (UMI, Ann Arbor)

Howard Bay: *Stage Design* (Pitman, London; Drama Book Publishers, New York)

Martin Friedman: *Hockney Paints The Stage* (Thames & Hudson, London)

John Goodwin (Ed.): *British Theatre Design — The Modern Age* (Weidenfeld & Nicolson, London)

Darwin Reid Payne: *Theory and Craft of the Scenographic Model* (Southern Illinois University Press, Carbondale)

John Willett: *Casper Neher — Brecht's Designer* (Methuen, London)

COSTUME DESIGN

Janet Arnold: *Patterns of Fashion* (Methuen, London)

Jean Hunnisett: *Period Costume for Stage and Screen* (Bell & Hyman, London)

Roy Strong et al: *Designing for the Dancer* (Elron Press)

THEATRE ARCHITECTURE

Michael Forsyth: *Auditoria Designing for the Performing Arts* (Batsford, London)

Roderick Ham: *Theatres — Planning Guidance for Design and Adaptation* (Architectural Press, London)

Richard Leacroft: *Theatre and Playhouse* (Methuen, London)

Richard Leacroft: *The Development of the English Playhouse* (Methuen, London)

Iain Mackintosh: *Architecture, Actor & Audience* (Routledge, London & New York)

Ronnie Mulryne & Margaret Shewring: *Making Space for Theatre — British Theatre Architecture since 1958* (Mulryne & Shewring, Stratford-upon-Avon)

THEATRE TECHNOLOGY

George C. Izenour: *Theatre Technology* (McGraw Hill)

Francis Reid: *The ABC of Stage Technology* (A & C Black, London; Heinemann, New Hampshire)

Graham Walne (Ed.): *Effects for the Theatre* (A & C Black, London; Drama Book Publishers, New York)

SCENE PAINTING

John Collins: *The Art of Scene Painting* (Harrap, London)

– If so, should we have realised beforehand and taken this into account in our designs and/or planning?
- How were the technical rehearsals?
  – Did the realised designs provide everything the director, choreographer and actors expected?
  – Were we flexible enough in developing ideas rather than just sticking too rigidly to the original?

How were our communications?

- Did the activities of the design team cause many surprises?
  – To each other?
  – To the rest of the production team?

Were we on schedule?

- Or did we try to do too much in the time available?

Were we within budget?

- If not, where did we miscalculate?

LIGHTING

Richard Pilbrow: *Stage Lighting* (Nick Hern Books, London; Drama Book Publishers, New York)

Francis Reid: *The A B C of Stage Lighting* (A & C Black, London; Drama Book Publishers, New York)

Francis Reid: *Discovering Stage Lighting* (Focal Press, London)

Francis Reid: *Lighting the Stage* (Focal Press, London)

Francis Reid: *The Stage Lighting Handbook* 4th edn (A & C Black, London; Routledge, New York)

Graham Walne: *Projection for the Performing Arts* (Focal Press, London)

STAGECRAFT & MANAGEMENT

Francis Reid: *The Staging Handbook* 2nd edn (A & C Black, London; Heinemann, New Hampshire)

PROPS

Jacquie Govier: *Create Your Own Stage Props* (A & C Black, London)

UNDERSTANDING THE PLAYWRIGHT

Simon Gray: *An Unnatural Pursuit* and *How's That For Telling 'Em, Fat Lady?* (Faber & Faber, London)

UNDERSTANDING THE ACTOR

Peter Barkworth: *About Acting* (Secker & Warburg, London)

Simon Callow: *Being An Actor* (Methuen, London)

Alec Guinness: *Blessings in Disguise* (Hamish Hamilton, London)

Anthony Sher: *The Year of the King* (Chatto & Windus, London)

UNDERSTANDING THE DIRECTOR

Peter Brook: *The Shifting Point* (Methuen, London)

Jonathan Miller: *Subsequent Performances* (Faber & Faber, London)

PRODUCTION DIARIES

Stephen Fay: *The Ring — Anatomy of an Opera* (Secker & Warburg, London)

Jim Hiley: *Theatre at Work — The Diary of the National Theatre's Production of Brecht's Galileo* (Routledge & Kegan Paul, London)

GLOSSARY OF TECHNICAL STAGE TERMS

Acting area The area of the stage setting within which the actor performs.
Alternative theatre Originally known as 'fringe theatre'. Aims to offer an experimental alternative to the more formal mainstream theatre and create a new audience in the process. The best of these alternative ideas and ideals are continuously being absorbed by mainstream theatre, allowing a fresh set of alternatives to develop.
Apron Part of the stage projecting towards or into the auditorium. In proscenium theatres, the part of the stage in front of the main house curtain.
Artistic director The person responsible for programme structure and performance standards.
ASM Assistant stage manager.

Backing (1) Piece of scenery behind a door, window, fireplace or similar opening. (2) The money invested in a commercial production.
Backlight Light coming from behind scenery or actors to sculpt and separate them from their background.
Battens (1) Lengths of timber at the tops and bottoms of cloths. (2) Timbers used for joining flats together ('battening out') for flying as 'French flats' (q.v.). (3) Lengths of overhead lighting floods arranged for colour mixing.
Beamlight Lensless spotlight giving intense parallel beam.
Black light UV (q.v.).
Bleed Lighting a scene behind a gauze to make the scene gradually visible through the gauze.
Book The storyline and words other than lyrics in a musical.
Boom Vertical pole, usually of scaffolding diameter, for mounting spotlights.
Borders Neutral or designed strips of material hung above the stage to form a limit to the scene and mask the technical regions above the performance area.
Box set Naturalistic setting of a complete room built from flats with only the side nearest the audience (the 'fourth wall') missing. Often complete with ceiling.
Brace Angled support for scenery. The standard adjustable-length brace hooks into a screw eye on the flat, and is either weighted to the floor or attached by a special large stage screw. See also *French brace*.
Brail To pull suspended scenery or lighting upstage or downstage from its natural free-hanging position by means of short rope lines attached to the end of the fly bar.
Breast To pull suspended scenery or lighting upstage or downstage from its free-hanging position by means of a rope line passed across the fly bar's suspension lines.
Bridge (1) An access catwalk, passing over the stage or incorporated within the auditorium ceiling, usually to facilitate spotlight focusing. (2) Elevators which raise and sink sections of a stage floor.

Build (1) To construct a scene from its component parts. (2) An increase in light intensity.

Bump out Australasian term for get-out (q.v.).

Bus and truck North American term for a tour specially designed for short stops (often one, two or three nights).

Call (1) A notification of a working session (e.g. rehearsal call). (2) A request for an actor to come to the stage because an entrance is imminent. (3) An acknowledgement of applause (i.e. curtain call).

Carpet cut A narrow trap along the front of the stage for clamping the downstage edge of a floorcloth.

Casuals Part-time temporary technicians.

Centre line Imaginary line running from front to back of the stage through the exact centre of the proscenium opening.

Cleat Special piece of timber or metal for tying off rope line — usually in the flys or on the back of a scenic flat.

Cloth A large area of scenic canvas hanging vertically. A *backcloth* completes the rear of a scene. A *frontcloth* hangs well downstage, often to hide a scene change taking place behind. *Cut cloths* have open areas and are normally used as a series, painted in perspective.

Commercial theatre Where production funding is supplied by investors who hope that it will be sufficiently successful at the box office not only to repay their capital but to distribute profits large enough to compensate for the high risk involved.

Counterweights Weights which are placed in the cradle of a flying system to counterbalance the weight of flown scenery.

Cue The signal that initiates a change of any kind, e.g. fly cue and light cue.

Cyclorama Plain cloth extending around and above the stage to give a feeling of infinite space. Term is often rather loosely used for any blue skycloth, either straight or with a limited curve at the ends.

Dark A theatre temporarily or permanently closed to the public.

Dead (1) The plotted height of a piece of suspended scenery or bar of lights (*trim* in America). (2) Discarded items of scenery.

Diffuser A filter, often called a *frost*, which softens the edge of a light beam.

Director Has the ultimate responsibility for the interpretation of the script through control of the actors and supporting production team.

Dock see *scene dock*.

Double handling Moving scenery or equipment more than necessary because it was not properly positioned in the first instance.

Double purchase Counterweight flying system where the cradle travels half the distance of the fly bar's travel and therefore leaves the side wall of the stage under the fly galleries clear of flying equipment.

Downstage The part of the stage nearest to the audience.

Dresser Helps actors with costume care and costume changing during the performance.

Dressing the house Selling seats in such a pattern that the auditorium looks fuller than it actually is.

Dressing (the set) Decorative (i.e. non-functional) items added to a stage setting.

Dress parade Prior to the first stage dress rehearsal, the actors wear each of their costumes in sequence so that director and designer can check the state of preparedness of the wardrobe department.

Drift The length of suspension wire between the counterweight bar and the top of the piece to be flown.

Dry An actor forgetting the words of the script.

Elevator stage Type of mechanical stage with sections which can be raised or lowered.

False proscenium A portal (q.v.), particularly one in the downstage area forming a designed frame for the action.

False stage A special stage floor laid for a production to allow trucks, guided by tracks cut into this false floor, to be moved by steel wires running in the shallow (5 or 8cm, 2 or 3in) void between the false and original stage floors.

Fit-up (1) Initial assembly on the stage of a production's hardware, including hanging scenery, building trucks, etc. (2) Installation of the production lighting (electrics fit-up).

Flats Lightweight timber frames covered with scenic canvas. Now usually covered with plywood and consequently no longer so lightweight.

Floats Jargon for footlights.

Fly bars The metal bars to which scenery and lights are attached for hoisting (i.e. flying) above the stage.

Fly floors High working platforms at the sides of the stage from which the flying lines are handled.

Flys Area above the stage into which scenery can be lifted out of sight of the audience.

Focusing Strictly speaking, the adjustment of lights to give a clearly defined image; but usually used to cover the whole process of adjusting the direction and beam of spotlights in which the desired image may be anything but clearly defined.

Follow spot Spotlight used with an operator so that the light beam can follow an actor around the stage.

French brace Timber non-adjustable brace (q.v.) usually attached to a scenic flat by a pin-hinge. Often swung flush to the flat on this hinge for packing or flying.

French flat A scenic flat which is flown into position.

Fringe see *alternative theatre*.

Front cloth (1) A cloth (q.v.) hanging at the front of the stage. (2) A variety act which can perform in the shallow depth of stage in front of a front cloth.

Frost A diffuser filter used to soften a light beam.

Gauze Fabric which becomes transparent or solid under appropriate lighting conditions (*scrim* in North America).

Get-in Unloading a production into the theatre.

Get-out (1) Dismantling a production and loading it into transport for removal from the theatre. (2) The minimum weekly box office receipts that will cover the production expenses to the point of breaking even.

Gobo A mask used in a profile spotlight for simple outline projection. Also used, with a softened focus, to texture the beam.

Green The part of the stage visible to the audience.

Green room Room adjacent to the stage (i.e. the green) for the actors to meet and relax.

Grid The arrangement of wooden or metal slats above which are mounted the pulley blocks of the flying system.

Gridded Any flying piece raised as high as possible into the flys, i.e. to the limit of travel of the flying lines.

Ground plan Plan showing the exact position of all items standing on the stage floor and indicating the position of items suspended above.

Groundrow A low piece of scenery standing on the stage floor. Also lengths of lighting placed on the stage floor.

Half Call given to the actors half an hour before they will be called to the stage for the beginning of the performance. Given 35 minutes before the advertised time of commencement. (Subsequent calls are 'the quarter', 'five' and 'beginners'.)

Hemp A rope used for flying. The term is generally used to cover all flying systems without counterweights.

Hemp house A theatre where the flying is brute-force manual without mechanical advantage from counterweights.

Industrial show A staged production to promote a product to the sales staff and agents of the manufacturing company.

Isora A plastic skycloth, lit from behind.

Ladder Framework in the shape of a ladder (but not climbable) for hanging side lighting.

Legs Vertical strips of fabric used mainly for masking.

Load out American term for get-out (q.v.).

Limes Jargon for follow spots (q.v.) and their operators.

Marking Placing small discreet marks on the stage floor (temporarily with tape, more permanently with paint) to aid the positioning of scenery and props during a change.

Marking out Sticking tapes to the rehearsal room floor to indicate the ground plan of the scenery.

Masking Neutral material or designed scenery which defines the performance area and conceals the technical areas.

Mechanist Alternative term (particularly Australasia) for technicians responsible for scenery handling.

Off An actor who misses an entrance.

O.P. 'Opposite prompt' side of the stage — stage right, i.e. actor's right when facing the audience.

Perches Lighting positions (often on platforms) at each side of the stage, immediately behind the proscenium.

Perruquier Specialist in making and/or dressing wigs.

Physical production The costs involved in providing all the material for the stage environment, i.e. the set building and painting, furniture and set-dressings, props, costumes.

Piano dress Rehearsal in costume and with all technical facilities but using piano as a substitute for orchestra so that the director can concentrate on movement and technical problems rather than musical ones.

Pin-hinge Hinge with removeable pin used to join two pieces of scenery together (i.e. one half of the hinge is on each piece of scenery).

Pipes North American term for the bars on which scenery or lights are flown.

Plot A listing of preparations and actions required during a performance. Each stage department prepares such plots as are required by the department's members.

Portal Framed masking border bolted to framed masking legs (q.v.), often given decorative treatment.

Practical Prop or light fitting which is not merely decorative but works or is wired to light up.

Preset Anything which is positioned in advance of its being required — such as props placed on the stage before the performance or a scene set behind a frontcloth, to be revealed when that cloth is flown.

Producer Formerly (and sometimes still in opera) the person who directed the actors. Now the packager who brings together script, theatre, production team, possibly the star(s) and certainly the money.

Production manager Responsible for the technical preparations, including budgeting and scheduling, of new productions.

Profile Shaped piece added to a scenery flat as an alternative to a straight edge.

Profile spot A spotlight which projects the outline (i.e. the *profile*) of any chosen shape and with any desired degree of hardness/softness (in North America often called *leko* or *ellipsoidal*).

Prompt book Master copy of the script or music score, containing all actor moves and technical cues, used by the stage management to control the performance.

Props (properties) Furnishings, set-dressings, and all items large and small which cannot be classified as scenery, electrics or wardrobe.

Proscenium theatre The traditional form of theatre where the audience sit in a single block facing the stage, with a fairly definite division between audience and stage. The position of this division is known as the *proscenium* and takes many forms from a definite arch, not unlike a picture frame, to an unstressed termination of the auditorium walls and ceiling.

P.S. 'Prompt side' of the stage — stage left, i.e. actor's left when facing the audience.

Repertoire A form of organisation where two or more productions alternate in the course of a week's performances.

Repertory A form of organisation, usually with a permanent company of actors, where each production has a run of limited length. At any time there is normally one production in performance, another in rehearsal and several in varying degrees of planning.

Repetiteur Pianist and vocal coach in an opera house.

Rim light Backlighting which creates a 'rim' of light around the actors to separate them from their background.

Riser (1) The vertical part of a step. (2) A microphone which can be raised through a small trap in the stage floor to a convenient height for an actor.

Road On tour.

Road manager (roadie) A touring technician with one-night-stands, particularly popular music groups.

Rostrum A portable platform usually in the form of a collapsible hinged framework with a separate top.

Run A sequence of performances of the same production.

Runners A pair of curtains parting at the centre and running horizontally, particularly those used in a downstage position in variety and revue productions.

Scene dock High-ceilinged storage area adjacent to the stage.

Scenographer The international term for the designer(s) who provide the visual environment for the actor. Implies a theatre where the environment is an integral constituent of the production rather than a decorative addition.

Scrim North American term for *gauze* (q.v.).

Segue Musical term for an immediate follow on. Often used as jargon for any kind of immediate follow on.

Shin busters Low level lights at stage floor level, used mainly for dance.

Sightlines Lines drawn on plan and section to indicate limits of audience vision from extreme seats, including side seats, front and back rows, and seats in galleries.

Single purchase Counterweight flying systems where the cradle travels the same distance as the fly bar's travel. The counterweight frame therefore occupies the full height of the side wall of the stage. See also *double purchase*.

Sitzprobe Opera house term for a rehearsal with orchestra where the cast sing but do not act.

Spot line A temporary line dropped from the grid to suspend something in an exact special position.

Staff director Member of staff in a repertoire theatre responsible for maintaining production standards, including revivals and cast changes. Usually was assistant director on the original rehearsals of the production.

Stage manager In overall control of the performance with responsibility for signalling the cues that co-ordinate the work of the actors and technicians. Some of this responsibility is delegated to the deputy stage manager (DSM) and assistant stage manager(s) (ASM).

Stage wait An interruption to the flow of the performance caused by an actor drying (q.v.), being off (q.v.), or a problem with a scene change.

Stagione A form of repertoire with a very small range of productions in performance at any given time. Each production is given intense rehearsal followed by a burst of performances close together, then placed in store. Revivals are rehearsed almost as if they were new productions.

Standing Scenery ('standing set') or lights ('standing light') which do not change during the performance.

Straight Non-musical — i.e. 'straight play', 'straight actor'.

Tabs Originally 'tableaux curtains' which drew outwards and upwards, but now generally applied to any curtain including a vertically flying front curtain (house tabs) and especially a pair of horizontally moving curtains which overlap at the centre and move outwards from that centre.

Tab-track Track with centre overlap for suspending and operating horizontally moving curtains.

Tallescope Alloy vertical ladder on an adjustable wheeled base.

Technical director (administrator/manager) Co-ordinates and budgets the work of all technical departments.

Theatre-in-the-round A form of staging where the audience totally encircle the acting area.

Throw Distance between a light and the actor or object being lit.

Thrust Form of stage which projects into the auditorium so that the audience are seated on at least two sides.

Topping and tailing Cutting out dialogue and action between cues in a technical rehearsal.

Tormentors Narrow masking flats adjacent and at right angles to the proscenium.

Transformation An instant scene change, often effected by exploiting the varying transparency of gauze under different lighting conditions.

Trim The height above stage level of a hanging piece of scenery, lights or masking. Mainly American (the equivalent in Britain is one of the meanings of *dead*).

Truck Castored platform on which a scene or part of a scene is built to facilitate scene changing.

Truss A framework of alloy bars and triangular cross-bracing (all of scaffolding diameter) providing a rigid structure, particularly useful for hanging lights.
Tumbling Flying a cloth from the bottom as well as from the top when there is insufficient height to fly in the normal way.

Upstage The part of the stage furthest from the audience.
UV Ultraviolet light (from which harmful radiations have been filtered out) used to light specially treated materials which fluoresce in an otherwise blackened stage.

Wagon stage Mechanised stage where the scenery is moved into position on large sliding platforms (as wide as the proscenium opening) from storage in large areas to the sides and rear of the main stage.
Wardrobe General name for the costume department, its staff and the accommodation that they occupy.
Wardrobe maintenance The division of the wardrobe department responsible for day-to-day cleaning, pressing and repairs.
Wardrobe plot Actor-by-actor, scene-by-scene inventory of all the costumes in a production, with a detailed breakdown into every separate item of each costume.
Wings (1) The technical areas to the sides of the acting area. (2) Scenery standing where the acting area joins these technical areas.
Wipe Single curtain moving across the stage on a single track (*wipe track*) rather than paired curtains on a tab-track (q.v.).

INDEX